LONGMAN
AMERICAN HISTORY ATLAS

Longman American History Atlas.

Copyright © 1999 Longman Publishers USA, a division of Addison Wesley Longman, Inc.

ISBN: 0-321-00486-8

CRC

04 05 10 9 8 7 6

CONTENTS

PREFACE

This atlas is designed to sit beside you as you study our nation's past. It belongs on your desk, next to a basic textbook, alongside a collection of interpretive readings or a set of primary source documents. These maps have been designed to hold a lot of information in an accessible manner. Most of them are unique to this volume and include parts of social history seldom seen geographically—like the history of ordinary settlers, Native Americans, and immigrants.

This atlas also tries to outline the whole continent of the United States—describing the settlement of Europeans as flowing not only from east-to-west but from north-to-south. For example, the settlement maps you'll find in six places in this atlas are designed to give you a snapshot of what the country looked like at a particular point in time—detailing the extent of European settlement, Native American groups, major transportation networks and economic patterns. In this way, this atlas has been created to give a comprehensive picture of our country and the people who have helped to make it what it is today.

This atlas has benefited from the help of eight subject specialists, all of whom teach the American history survey course <u>and</u> have an abiding interest in maps. These experts, on subjects as diverse as World War I, western history, and African Americans, have examined all the maps in this atlas and helped us create a resource which is as historically accurate as it is easy to understand.

Geography has been immensely important in the history of the United States. It has helped determine where settlers survived and where they encountered disease, where railroads were laid and where canals seemed more appropriate, where cities have thrived and where agriculture is king. You can use this atlas to learn about the history and geography of this country in five general ways—the first one is the easiest.

Locating Places

When you come across a place and do not know where it is located, you can turn to the index of this atlas and find the page on which it appears. If it is a city or a town, the locator symbol such as A1 or H7 will tell you where to find this mysterious place on the appropriate map. Each map is divided into an imaginary grid. The columns running up and down on the map are assigned a number, starting at the left. In the same way, each row of blocks running along the top has a letter of the alphabet. Thus a place located in A1 would be at the top left of the map while H7 would direct your search to the lower right. For example, the battle of Antietam will be located on page 29, in block number E7.

Reading Historical Maps

An atlas is more than just a place-finding tool. All maps are more than just tables showing locations. They are living creations and tell stories. We've taken great pains to avoid cluttering the maps in this atlas so that each one can tell its story in a straightforward way.

Reading the title of each map is the best way to start reading the map. What historical moment is the central theme of this map? Then look at the area covered, noting how insets often highlight particular regions in greater detail. Carefully note the legend which provides the key to the symbols used by the cartographer. Why were these data chosen and not others? How does the information provided tell a story? When did the story take place? What changes over time are indicated on the map? What questions or connections are suggested by other data available on the map?

Asking a regular sequence of questions is a good way to get started reading any document. Another way is to read the captions underneath the map. Each of these little paragraphs starts with a general observation providing context for the subject at hand. Then every caption asks a question to inspire analysis of the map.

Pre-reading

This atlas is very useful when used in conjunction with a textbook which surveys the course of American history. Looking at one or two pertinent maps before turning to a chapter might be a good way to begin a study session. For example, looking at the maps on pages 25 through 34 might be a good prelude to reading about Secession and the Civil War—they'll help you see how the North and South were differently equipped to fight a war and will give you some information to see how the war affected both sides of the country. Spending a few minutes analyzing the map provides a geographic context and a conceptual vocabulary that help set up the chapter. Beginning any assignment with an appropriate frame of reference is bound to pay handsome dividends.

Geographic Roots

This atlas can play an active role in your study of history by serving as a manual to root the historical events in geography. Anchoring history in particular places is a central function of historical geography. History always changes but locations are a constant element. The maps you should look at first in this atlas are those that begin it— the maps which describe the topography of this continent. These topographical features are what hold the narrative together.

Reflections

Maps can also be used after you've learned about a period to help reflect on how each period in history is connected to the general course of historical development. Reflection is a quest for meaning, a "bending back:" trying to fit a specific event into the general flow of time. But Clio, the muse of history, is not a tidy person. The general synthesis that she offers never fits exactly. Maps have a way of intimating that we do not know the full story.

No map can answer all the questions that it raises. Maps never reach an end, always suggest other dimensions beyond the page, just off the edge of the sheet. Ideally, they should help us to see that history is more inquiry than resolution. We hope that this atlas will encourage you to actively engage the past as you seek to understand it. We wish you well on your adventure and send along these maps to sit beside you.

We wish to thank all the people who have been involved in the development of this project. This has been a very collaborative effort and we are thankful for the feedback from the following people: David R. Buck, West Virginia University; Kathleen Carter, High Point University; Debbie Kaspar, Clatsop Community College; Richard Francaviglia, University of Texas at Arlington; Rita E. Loos, Framingham State College; and Bill Paquette, Tidewater College.

Gerald A. Danzer
University of Illinois at Chicago

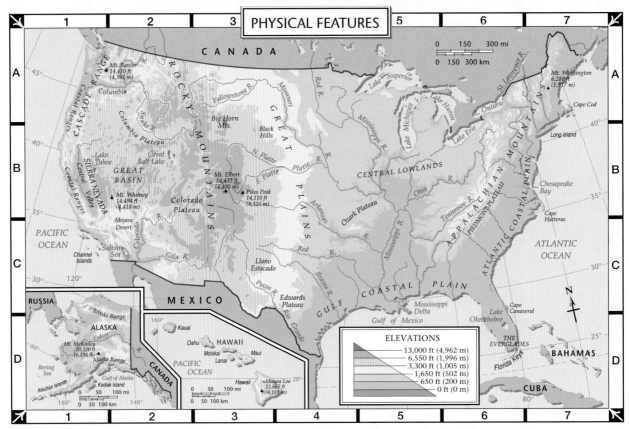

PHYSICAL FEATURES

Bounded by two oceans, the United States encompasses a varied range of topography including mountain ranges, coastal lowlands, arid plains, tropical islands, and countless lakes and rivers. About which portion of the contiguous forty-eight states is drained by the Mississippi River and its tributaries?

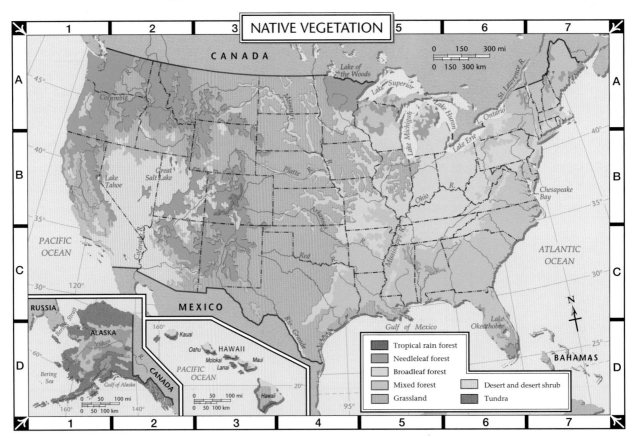

NATIVE VEGETATION

The diversity of America's native vegetation gives each region a particular character. The East is largely dominated by mixed forests of needleleaf (coniferous) and broadleaf (deciduous) trees; forests gradually give way to grasslands in the Midwest; and the Far West exhibits a mixture of forest, grassland, and desert. The northernmost state, Alaska, includes vast expanses of tundra; while to the south, the Hawaiian Islands have both tropical forests and grasslands. How has the diversity of ecosystems influenced the development of the American nation?

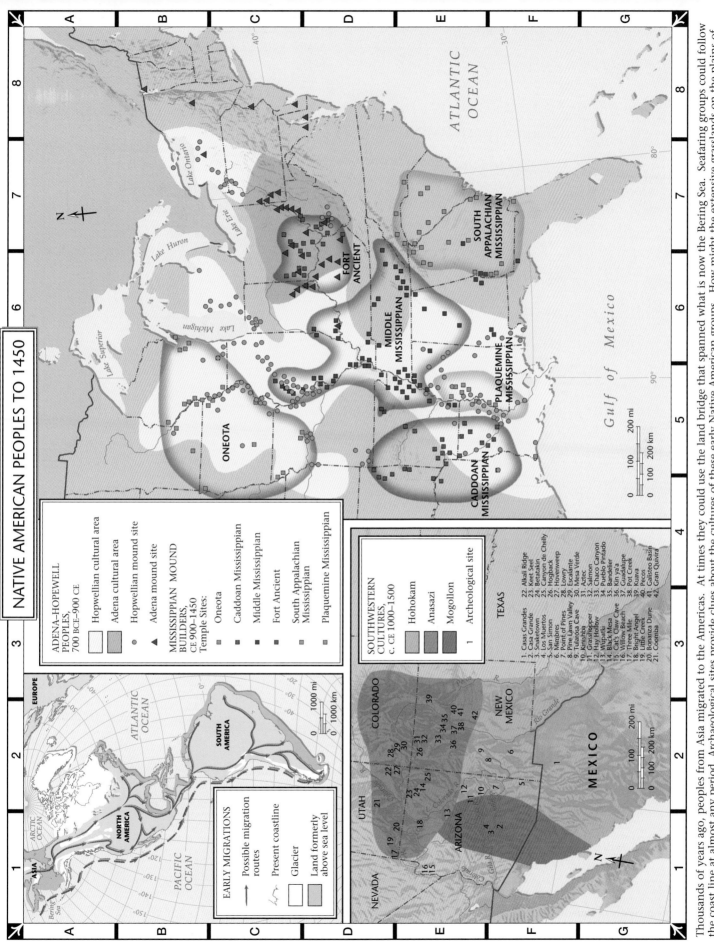

NATIVE AMERICAN PEOPLES TO 1450

ADENA–HOPEWELL PEOPLES, 700 BCE–900 CE
- Hopwellian cultural area
- Adena cultural area
- ● Hopwellian mound site
- ▲ Adena mound site

MISSISSIPPIAN MOUND BUILDERS, CE 900–1450
Temple Sites:
- ■ Oneota
- ■ Caddoan Mississippian
- ■ Middle Mississippian
- ■ Fort Ancient
- ■ South Appalachian Mississippian
- ■ Plaquemine Mississippian

EARLY MIGRATIONS
- → Possible migration routes
- ⌇ Present coastline
- Glacier
- Land formerly above sea level

SOUTHWESTERN CULTURES, c. CE 1000–1500
- Hohokam
- Anasazi
- Mogollon
- 1 Archeological site

1. Casa Grandes
2. Casa Grande
3. Snaketown
4. Los Muertos
5. San Simon
6. Mimbres
7. Point of Pines
8. Pine Lawn Valley
9. Tularosa Cave
10. Mesa Verde
11. Grasshopper
12. Hay Hollow
13. Wupatki
14. Black Mesa
15. Cat's Claw Cave
16. Willow Beach
17. Three Mile
18. Bright Angel
19. Little Creek
20. Bonanza Dune
21. Coombs
22. Alkali Ridge
23. Keet Seel
24. Kietatakin
25. Canyon de Chelly
26. Hogback
27. Hoventweep
28. Lowry
29. Escalante
30. Mesa Verde
31. Aztec
32. Salmon
33. Chaco Canyon
34. Pueblo Pintado
35. Bandelier
36. Kin ya'a
37. Guadalupe
38. Pot Creek
39. Kuava
40. Pecos
41. Calisteo Basin
42. Gran Quivira

Thousands of years ago, peoples from Asia migrated to the Americas. At times they could follow the coast line at almost any period. Seafaring groups could follow the Bering Sea. Archaeological sites provide clues about the cultures of these early Native American groups. How might the extensive grasslands on the plains of North America have encouraged the wide dispersal of people in a relatively brief time?

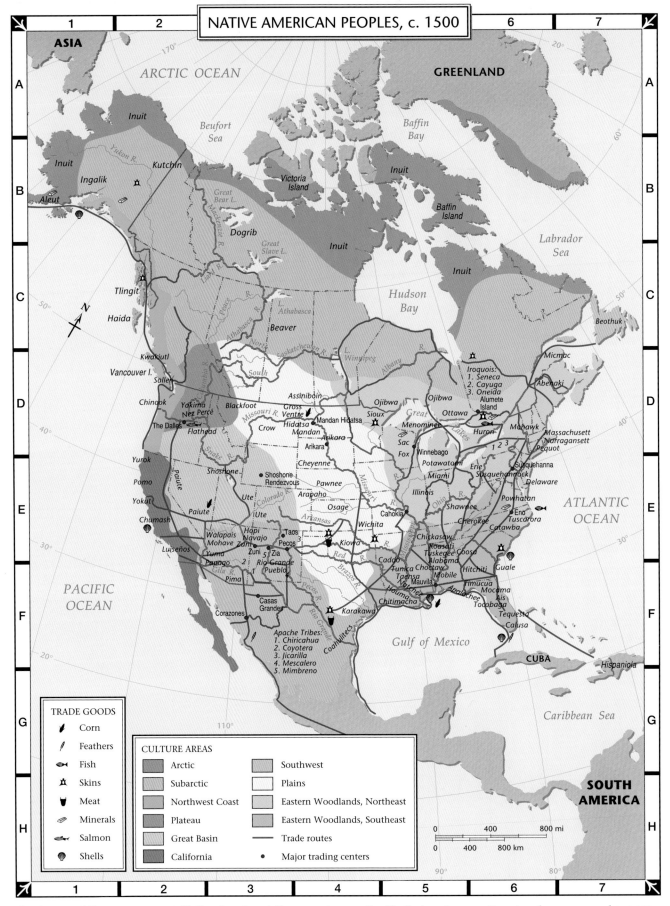

NATIVE AMERICAN PEOPLES, c. 1500

ASIA

ARCTIC OCEAN

GREENLAND

Beufort Sea

Baffin Bay

Inuit

Inuit

Kutchin

Ingalik

Aleut

Victoria Island

Inuit

Baffin Island

Labrador Sea

Tlingit

Haida

Dogrib

Great Bear L.

Great Slave L.

Inuit

Hudson Bay

Inuit

Beothuk

Kwakiutl

Vancouver I.

Salleh

Beaver

Micmac

Iroquois:
1. Seneca
2. Cayuga
3. Oneida
Alumete Island

Abenaki

Chinook

Yakima

Nez Percé

The Dalles

Blackfoot

Gross Ventre

Mandan Hidatsa

Ojibwa

Ojibwa

Ottawa

Huron

Mohawk

Flathead

Crow

Hidatsa

Mandan

Arikara

Sioux

Menominee

Massachusett
Narragansett
Pequot

Yurok

Pomo

Yokut

Chumash

Paiute

Shoshone

Shoshone Rendezvous

Cheyenne

Pawnee

Arapaho

Sac Fox

Winnebago

Potawatomi

Miami

Illinois

Erie

Susquehanna

Susquehannock

Delaware

Luiseños

Walapais
Mohave

Hopi
Navajo
Zuni

Ute

Ute

Osage

Cahokia

Wichita

Shawnee

Cherokee

Powhatan

Eno

Tuscarora

Catawba

ATLANTIC OCEAN

Yuma
Papago

Zuni

Taos

Pecos

Zia

Rio Grande
Pueblo

Kiowa

Caddo

Chickasaw

Koasati
Tuskegee
Alabama

Coosa

Pima

Tunica

Taensa

Choctaw

Mobile

Hitchiti

Guale

Casas Grandes

Houma

Natchez

Mauvila

Corazones

Apache Tribes:
1. Chiricahua
2. Coyotera
3. Jicarilla
4. Mescalero
5. Mimbreno

Karakawa

Coahuiltecs

Chitimacha

Timucua

Mocoma

Ais

Tocobaga

Appalachee

Tequesta

Calusa

PACIFIC OCEAN

Gulf of Mexico

CUBA

Hispaniola

Caribbean Sea

SOUTH AMERICA

TRADE GOODS

- Corn
- Feathers
- Fish
- Skins
- Meat
- Minerals
- Salmon
- Shells

CULTURE AREAS

- Arctic
- Subarctic
- Northwest Coast
- Plateau
- Great Basin
- California
- Southwest
- Plains
- Eastern Woodlands, Northeast
- Eastern Woodlands, Southeast
- Trade routes
- Major trading centers

0   400   800 mi
0   400   800 km

On the eve of European contact, Native American tribes spread across the North American continent and encompassed a range of different cultures, languages, and religious beliefs. Trade goods exchanged between these diverse groups furnished avenues of communication across the continent. What geographic features presented barriers to trade according to this map?

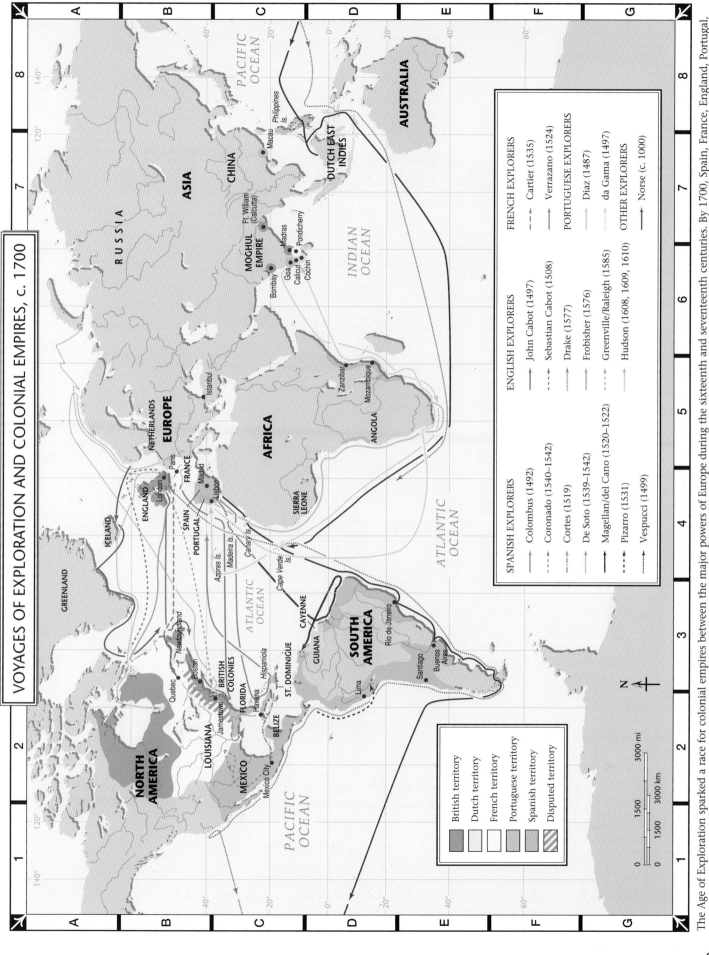

VOYAGES OF EXPLORATION AND COLONIAL EMPIRES, c. 1700

SPANISH EXPLORERS
→ Colombus (1492)
┄→ Coronado (1540–1542)
┅→ Cortes (1519)
┈→ De Soto (1539–1542)
→ Magellan/del Cano (1520–1522)
┅→ Pizarro (1531)
┈→ Vespucci (1499)

ENGLISH EXPLORERS
→ John Cabot (1497)
┄→ Sebastian Cabot (1508)
┈→ Drake (1577)
→ Frobisher (1576)
┅→ Greenville/Raleigh (1585)
┈→ Hudson (1608, 1609, 1610)

FRENCH EXPLORERS
┄→ Cartier (1535)
→ Verrazano (1524)

PORTUGUESE EXPLORERS
→ Diaz (1487)
→ da Gama (1497)

OTHER EXPLORERS
→ Norse (c. 1000)

British territory
Dutch territory
French territory
Portuguese territory
Spanish territory
Disputed territory

N

0	1500	3000 mi	
0	1500	3000 km	

The Age of Exploration sparked a race for colonial empires between the major powers of Europe during the sixteenth and seventeenth centuries. By 1700, Spain, France, England, Portugal, and the Netherlands had divided up the Americas and established claims in Africa and Asia. Why were there so few European colonies in Africa compared to the Americas in 1700?

SPANISH AMERICA, TO 1610

| | 1 | 2 | 3 | 4 | 5 | 6 | 7 |

Taos (1609)
Sante Fe (1609)
Colorado R.
Río Grande
Mississippi R.
St. Augustine (1565)
SPANISH FLORIDA
San Pedro de Lagunas (1590)
San Miguel de Aguayo (1532)
Gulf of Mexico
La Habana (1522)
Nombre de Dios (1555)
Culicán (1533)
Mexico City (Tenochtitlán) (1521)
Veracruz (1519)
Puerto Rico (1502)
Santo Domingo (1496)
VICE-ROYALTY OF NEW SPAIN
Guatemala (1519)
Caribbean Sea
Panama (1519)
Caracas (1567)
Trinidad (1498)
Orinoco R.
Magdalena R.
Santa Fe de Bogotá (1538)
VICE-ROYALTY OF NEW GRANADA
ATLANTIC OCEAN
Equator
Quito (1534)
Amazon R.
Negro R.
PACIFIC OCEAN
Ciudad de los Reyes (Lima) (1538)
Cuzco (1535)
VICE-ROYALTY OF PERU
La Paz (1548)
Sucre (1540)
Potosí (1546)
Paraguay R.
Treaty of Tordesillas (1494)
São Francisco R.
PORTUGUESE BRAZIL
São Paulo (1554)
Rio de Janeiro (1565)
Paraná R.
Valparaiso (1544)
Santiago (1541)
VICE-ROYALTY OF LA PLATA
Buenos Aires (1535)
ATLANTIC OCEAN

N

Legend

- Inca Empire at the time of the Spanish Conquest
- Aztec Empire at the time of Spanish Conquest
- Portuguese settlements
- British settlements
- Spanish settlements
- Missions
- • Settlements
- (1521) Date of settlement

0 200 400 mi
0 200 400 km

120° 110° 100° 90° 80° 70° 60° 50° 40° 30° 20°
30° 20° 10° 0° 10° 20° 30° 40° 50°

The Spanish were the first to establish a colonial empire in the New World, with missions and settlements extending north into the American Southwest, and south into present-day Chile. In the process, Spain subdued two major Native American empires, the Aztec and the Inca, and outflanked from their European rival, Portugal. Over how many degrees of latitude did the Spanish Empire extend in the Americas? What problems might this have led to in governing such diverse and expansive lands?

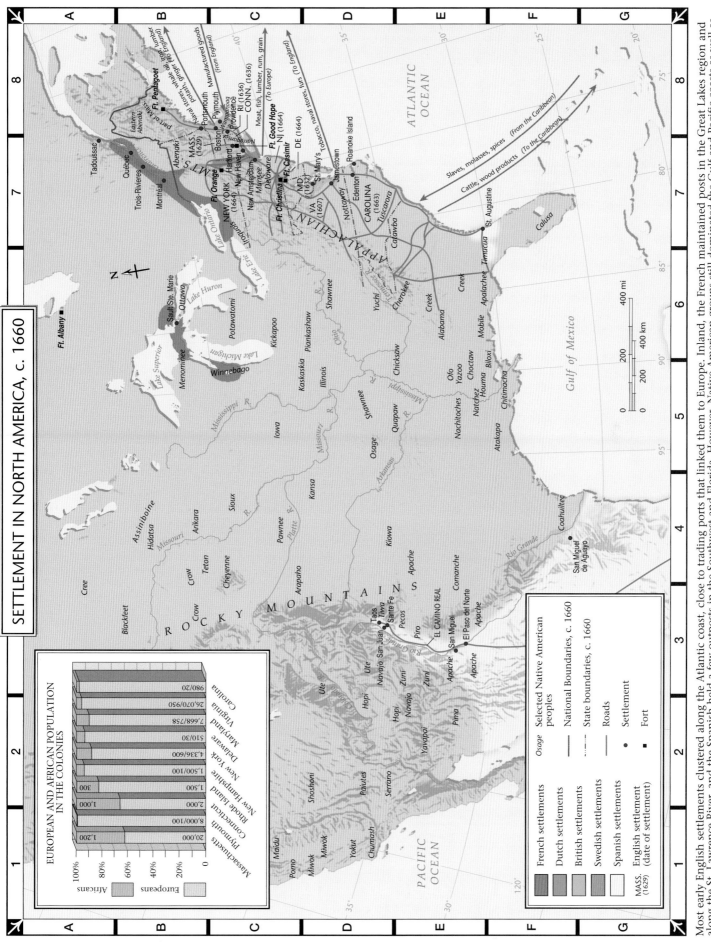

SETTLEMENT IN NORTH AMERICA, c. 1660

EUROPEAN AND AFRICAN POPULATION IN THE COLONIES

Colony	Africans	Europeans
Massachusetts	1,200	20,000
Plymouth	—	1,500
Connecticut	300	8,000/100
Rhode Island	—	1,000
New Hampshire	—	1,500
New York	600	4,336/600
Delaware	—	510/30
Maryland	758	7,668/758
Virginia	950	26,070/950
Carolina	20	980/20

Legend:
- French settlements
- Dutch settlements
- British settlements
- Swedish settlements
- Spanish settlements
- MASS. (1629) English settlement (date of settlement)

- *Osage* Selected Native American peoples
- —— National Boundaries, c. 1660
- ------ State boundaries, c. 1660
- —— Roads
- • Settlement
- ■ Fort

Trade arrows and labels:
- Naval stores, whale oil, lumber (To England)
- Manufactured goods (from England)
- Meat, fish, lumber, rum, grain (To Europe)
- Tobacco, naval stores, furs (To England)
- Slaves, molasses, spices (From the Caribbean)
- Cattle, wood products (To the Caribbean)

Scale: 400 mi / 400 km

Most early English settlements clustered along the Atlantic coast, close to trading ports that linked them to Europe. Inland, the French maintained posts in the Great Lakes region and along the St. Lawrence River, and the Spanish held a few outposts in the Southwest and Florida. However, Native American groups still dominated the Gulf and Pacific coasts as well as the vast interior. To which areas would you expect the French to extend their control in the eighteenth century?

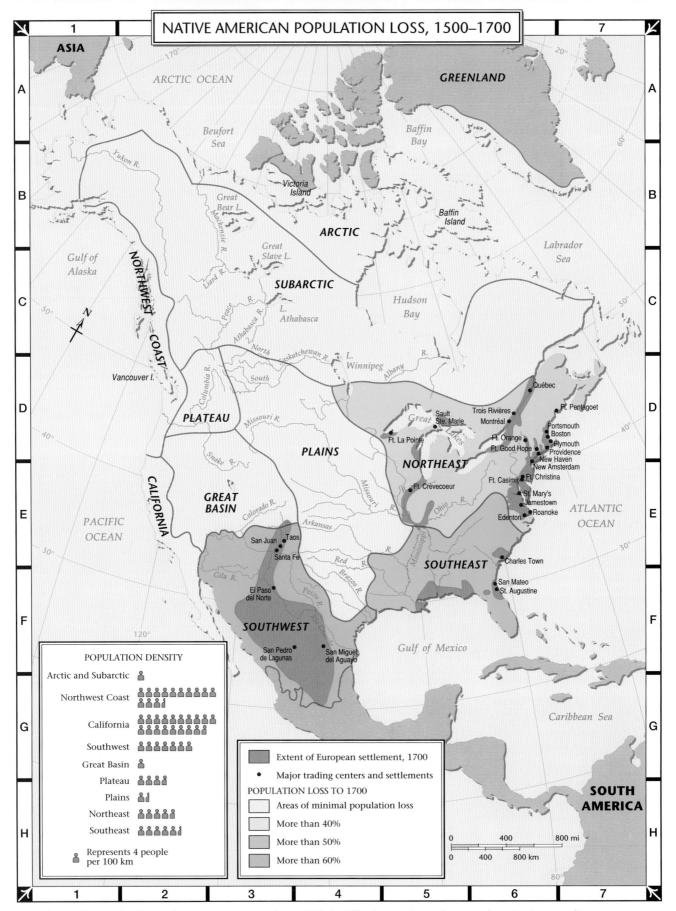

POPULATION DENSITY

Arctic and Subarctic
Northwest Coast
California
Southwest
Great Basin
Plateau
Plains
Northeast
Southeast

Represents 4 people
per 100 km

Extent of European settlement, 1700

• Major trading centers and settlements

POPULATION LOSS TO 1700

Areas of minimal population loss

More than 40%

More than 50%

More than 60%

Population density for Native American groups at about 1500 is difficult to estimate because there is vigorous disagreement among scholars about the size of America's population just before European contact. There is also much uncertainty about the area that should be assigned to each culture area. Does this map suggest that distance from the points of European contact was also an important variable in determining population loss in various culture areas?

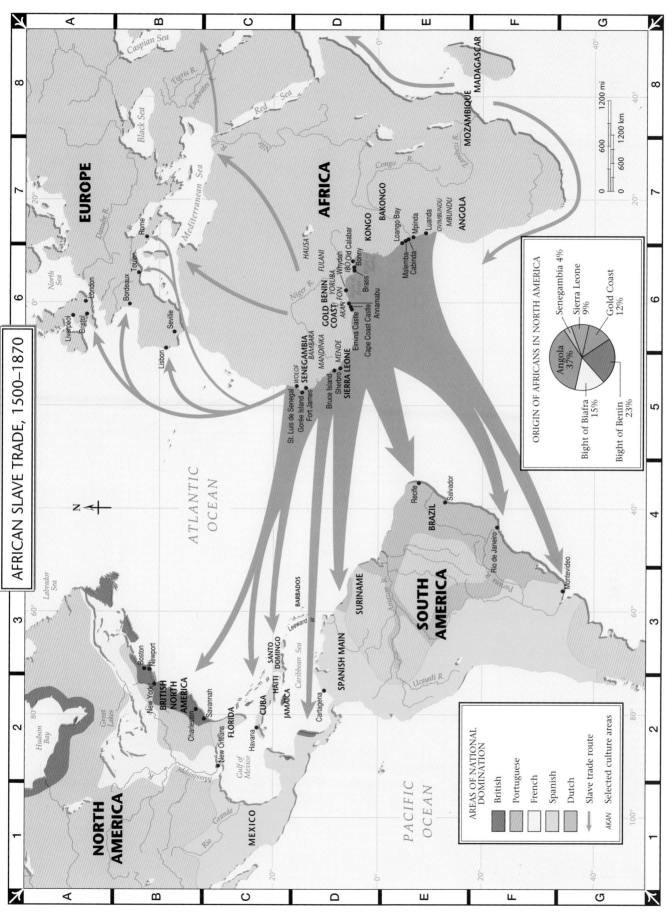

AFRICAN SLAVE TRADE, 1500–1870

NORTH AMERICA

EUROPE

AFRICA

SOUTH AMERICA

ATLANTIC OCEAN

PACIFIC OCEAN

Labrador Sea

Hudson Bay

Great Lakes

Boston
Newport
New York
BRITISH NORTH AMERICA
Charleston
Savannah
New Orleans
FLORIDA

Gulf of Mexico
Havana
CUBA
SANTO DOMINGO
HAITI
JAMAICA
Caribbean Sea
BARBADOS
Leeward Is.
Cartagena
SPANISH MAIN
SURINAME

MEXICO
Rio Grande

Mississippi

BRAZIL
Recife
Salvador
Rio de Janeiro
Montevideo

Amazon R.
Ucayali R.
Parana R.

North Sea
Liverpool
Bristol
London
Bordeaux
Toulon
Rome
Lisbon
Seville

Danube R.
Caspian Sea
Black Sea
Mediterranean Sea
Tigris R.
Euphrates
Red Sea
Nile

St. Luis de Senegal
Gorée Island
Fort James
SENEGAMBIA
WOLOF
BAMBARA
MANDINKA
Bruce Island
MENDE
Sherbro
SIERRA LEONE
Elmina Castle
Cape Coast Castle
GOLD BENIN
COAST
AKAN
FON
YORUBA
IBO Old Calabar
Whydah
Bonny
Brass
Annamabu
HAUSA
FULANI

Niger R.
Congo R.
Zambezi R.

Loango Bay
Malemba
Cabinda
Mpinda
Luanda
BAKONGO
KONGO
OVIMBUNDU
MBUNDU
ANGOLA

MOZAMBIQUE
MADAGASCAR

AREAS OF NATIONAL DOMINATION

- British
- Portuguese
- French
- Spanish
- Dutch
- → Slave trade route
- *AKAN* Selected culture areas

ORIGIN OF AFRICANS IN NORTH AMERICA

- Senegambia 4%
- Sierra Leone 9%
- Gold Coast 12%
- Bight of Benin 23%
- Bight of Biafra 15%
- Angola 37%

Scale: 0 — 600 — 1200 mi / 0 — 600 — 1200 km

N

After claiming territories in the New World, Europeans looked for profitable ways of developing their holdings. In North America, landowners growing popular cash crops such as tobacco, rice, and indigo turned to the use of African slaves. Millions of Africans from diverse cultural groups were sold to slave traders on the West Coast of Africa between 1600 and 1800. In all, some 400,000 Africans survived the voyage to British North America during the duration of the slave trade; millions more were transported to planta-tions in Latin America and the Caribbean. Did the African diaspora have a similar effect on the various regions of the Americas?

13

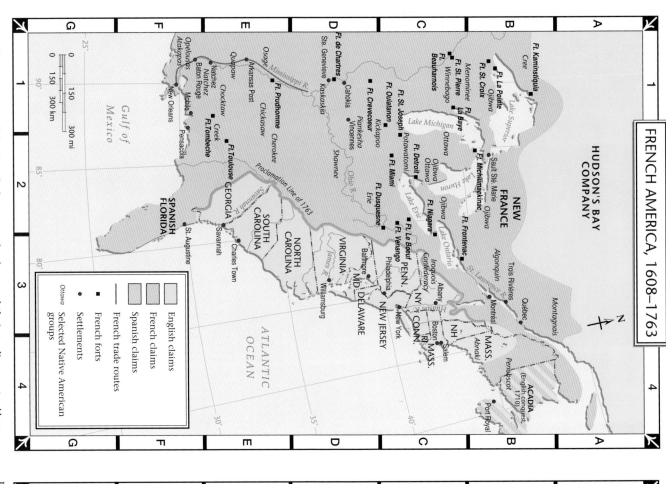

FRENCH AMERICA, 1608–1763

HUDSON'S BAY COMPANY

NEW FRANCE

Cree
Ft. Kaministiquia
Ft. La Pointe
Ojibwa
Lake Superior
Menominee
Ft. St. Pierre
Ft. St. Croix
Ojibwa
Winnebago
Ft. La Baye
Ft. Beauharnois
Sault Ste. Marie
Ft. Michilimackinac
Ojibwa
Ottawa
Lake Michigan
Ottawa
Ottawa
Ojibwa
Lake Huron
Ft. Detroit
Ft. Miami
Potawatomi
Erie
Ft. Dusquesne
Lake Erie
Ft. Niagara
Ft. Le Boeuf
Ft. Venango
Lake Ontario
Iroquois Confederacy
St. Lawrence R.
Québec
Trois Rivières
Montréal
Algonquin
Montagnais

Osage
Quapaw
Ft. Prudhomme
Ft. St. Joseph
Ft. Ouiatanon
Kickapoo
Ft. Crevecoeur
Cahokia
Vincennes
Piankesha
Shawnee
Ohio R.
Kaskaskia
Ste. Geneviève
Ft. de Chartres
Arkansas Post
Chickasaw
Cherokee
Proclamation Line of 1763
GEORGIA
SOUTH CAROLINA
NORTH CAROLINA
VIRGINIA
Savannah R.
James R.
Williamsburg
Baltimore
MD.
DELAWARE
PENN.
Philadelphia
N.J.
New York
CONN.
N.Y.
Albany
Boston
MASS.
R.I.
N.H.
Salem
MASS.
Abnaki
Penobscot
ACADIA (English conquest, 1710)
Port Royal

Mississippi R.
New Orleans
Mobile
Pensacola
Baton Rouge
Natchez
Chockraw
Creek
Ft. Tombeche
Ft. Toulouse
Atakapas
Opelousas
Gulf of Mexico
SPANISH FLORIDA
St. Augustine
Charles Town

ATLANTIC OCEAN

Legend:
English claims
Spanish claims
French claims
French trade routes
French forts ■
Settlements ●
Ottawa Selected Native American groups

French power west of the Appalachians revolved around their trading posts. Along the St. Lawrence River and in the lower Mississippi River, they had a more permanent presence, possessing strong administrative, agricultural, and military institutions. Why were there no French forts or settlements on the Ohio River?

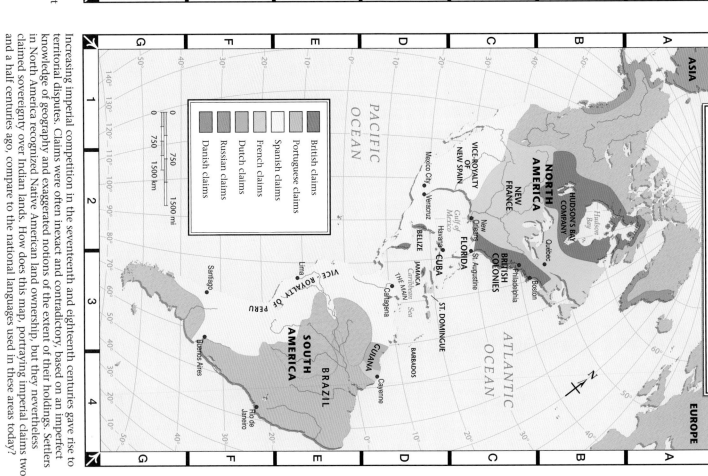

EUROPEAN CLAIMS IN AMERICA, c. 1750

ASIA
EUROPE
PACIFIC OCEAN
ATLANTIC OCEAN

NORTH AMERICA
HUDSON'S BAY COMPANY
Hudson Bay
NEW FRANCE
Québec
Philadelphia
Boston
BRITISH COLONIES
VICE-ROYALTY OF NEW SPAIN
Mexico City
Veracruz
Gulf of Mexico
New Orleans
FLORIDA
St. Augustine
Havana
CUBA
JAMAICA
BELIZE
THE MAIN
Caribbean Sea
ST. DOMINGUE
BARBADOS
Cartagena
GUIANA
Cayenne

Lima
VICE-ROYALTY OF PERU
Santiago
SOUTH AMERICA
BRAZIL
Buenos Aires
Rio de Janeiro

Legend:
British claims
Portuguese claims
Spanish claims
French claims
Dutch claims
Russian claims
Danish claims

Increasing imperial competition in the seventeenth and eighteenth centuries gave rise to territorial disputes. Claims were often inexact and contradictory, based on an imperfect knowledge of geography and exaggerated notions of the extent of their holdings. Settlers in North America recognized Native American land ownership, but they nevertheless claimed sovereignty over Indian lands. How does this map, portraying imperial claims two and a half centuries ago, compare to the national languages used in these areas today?

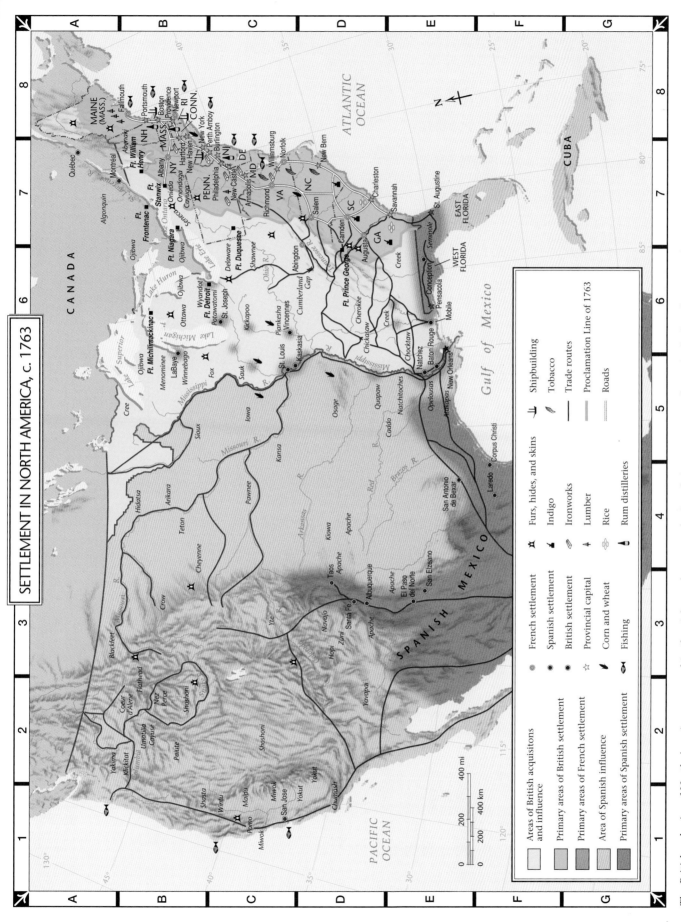

SETTLEMENT IN NORTH AMERICA, c. 1763

Legend:

- ⊙ French settlement
- ⊙ Spanish settlement
- ● British settlement
- ☆ Provincial capital
- 🌾 Corn and wheat
- 🐟 Fishing

- ⚓ Furs, hides, and skins
- 🍂 Indigo
- ▰ Ironworks
- ✿ Lumber
- 🌾 Rice
- 🍶 Rum distilleries

- ⚓ Shipbuilding
- 🍃 Tobacco
- — Trade routes
- — Proclamation Line of 1763
- ⚍ Roads

- Areas of British acquisitons and influence
- Primary areas of British settlement
- Primary areas of French settlement
- Area of Spanish influence
- Primary areas of Spanish settlement

Scale: 0   200   400 mi
0   200   400 km

The British colonies of North America prospered in the eighteenth century, basing their economy on the region's abundant natural resources. As settlers increasingly moved west in search of undeveloped land, the British government established the Proclamation Line of 1763 to delineate lands reserved for the Native Americans. Both the French and the Spanish had established a few settlements across the Appalachian Mountains focusing primarily on the fur trade. Which empire seems to be more extended in North America in 1763, Spain or Britain? Why?

15

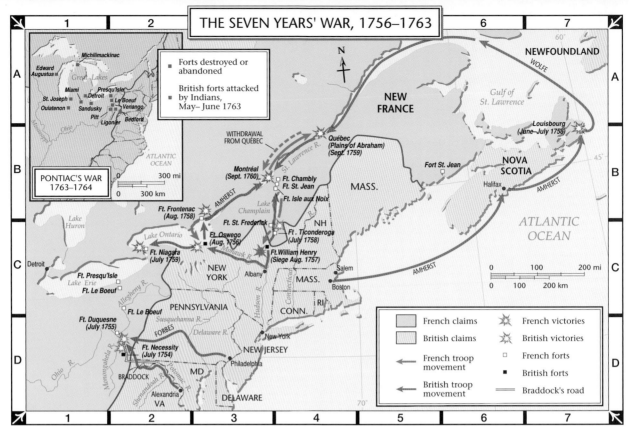

THE SEVEN YEARS' WAR, 1756–1763

Territorial ambitions in North America finally led to war between Great Britain and France. The Seven Years' War is often remembered in America as the French and Indian War, as many Native Americans sided with the French. Despite initial defeats, the British troops and American colonists won decisive victories on the St. Lawrence River. Peace was declared in 1763 but conflict continued in the West where Native American tribes inspired by Pontiac attacked British forts and settlements. The axis between Quebec and Montreal has been compared to a trunk which supported the great crown of France's empire, extending from New Orleans to Lake Superior. How does this observation explain British strategy in 1759-1760?

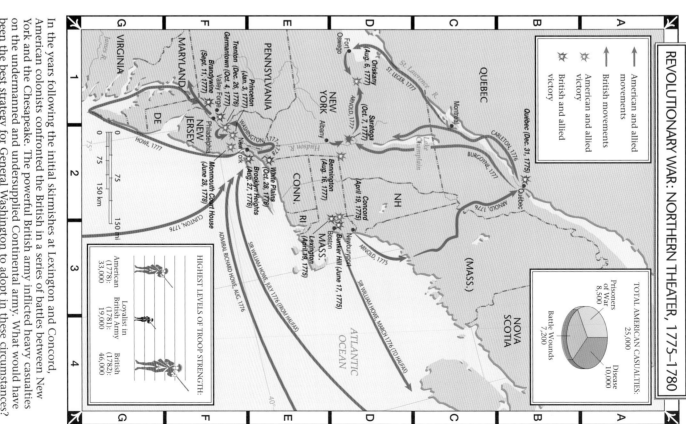

REVOLUTIONARY WAR: NORTHERN THEATER, 1775-1780

In the years following the initial skirmishes at Lexington and Concord, American colonists confronted the British in a series of battles between New York and the Chesapeake. The powerful British army inflicted heavy casualties on the undermanned and undersupplied Continental army. What would have been the best strategy for General Washington to adopt in these circumstances?

16

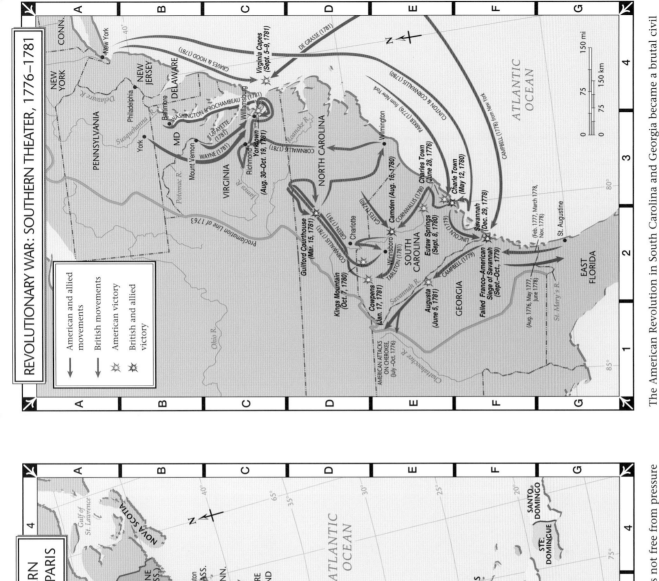

REVOLUTIONARY WAR: SOUTHERN THEATER, 1776–1781

Legend:
→ American and allied movements
→ British movements
✦ American victory
✦ British and allied victory

Labels on map:
NEW YORK
CONN.
New York
NEW JERSEY
PENNSYLVANIA
Philadelphia
York
Baltimore
DELAWARE
MD
Mount Vernon
WASHINGTON & ROCHAMBEAU (1781)
WAYNE (1781)
LAFAYETTE (1781)
Williamsburg (1781)
Richmond
Yorktown (Aug. 30–Oct. 19, 1781)
VIRGINIA
CORNWALLIS (1781)
Proclamation Line of 1763
Ohio R.
Potomac R.
Susquehanna R.
Delaware R.
James R.
Roanoke R.
GRAVES & HOOD (1781)
Virginia Capes (Sept. 5–9, 1781)
DE GRASSE (1781)
N
NORTH CAROLINA
Wilmington
CLINTON & CORNWALLIS (1780) from New York
PARKER (1776) from New York
CAMPBELL (1778) from New York
ATLANTIC OCEAN
Guilford Courthouse (Mar. 15, 1781)
Charlotte
GATES (1780)
CORNWALLIS (1780)
Camden (Aug. 16, 1780)
Charles Town (June 28, 1776)
Charle Town (May 12, 1780)
GREENE (1781)
CORNWALLIS (1781)
Kings Mountain (Oct. 7, 1780)
Cowpens (Jan. 17, 1781)
TARLETON (1781)
SOUTH CAROLINA
Winnsboro
Eutaw Springs (Sept. 8, 1780)
LINCOLN (1779)
Savannah (Dec. 29, 1778)
Augusta (June 5, 1781)
Savannah R.
Chattahoochee R.
CAMPBELL (1779)
GEORGIA
Failed Franco-American Siege of Savannah (Sept.–Oct., 1779)
(Feb. 1777, March 1778, Nov. 1778)
St. Augustine
EAST FLORIDA
(Aug. 1776, May 1777, June 1778)
St. Mary's R.
AMERICAN ATTACKS ON CHEROKEE, (July–Oct. 1776)
40°
80°
85°

Scale:
0   75   150 mi
0   75   150 km

The American Revolution in South Carolina and Georgia became a brutal civil war, where competing British and American governments were unable to maintain authority over militias, bandits, and a vicious cycle of vengeance among rebels and loyalists. Trace the route taken by the army commanded by Cornwallis in 1780-1781. Why did it have so little to show for its long march in August, 1781?

TERRITORIAL CLAIMS IN EASTERN AMERICA AFTER THE TREATY OF PARIS

Legend:
British claims
United States claims
Spanish claims
French claims
• Settlement

Labels on map:
BRITISH CANADA
Gulf of St. Lawrence
NOVA SCOTIA
Québec
Montréal
VERMONT (claimed by NY and NH)
MAINE (MASS.)
NH
MASS.
Boston
RI
CONN.
New York
NEW YORK
NEW JERSEY
Philadelphia
PENN.
DELAWARE
MARYLAND
Norfolk
VIRGINIA
Fort Niagara
Lake Ontario
Lake Erie
Lake Huron
Lake Michigan
Lake Superior
Fort Detroit
Ohio R.
Boonesboro
Harrodsburg
Nashville
NORTH CAROLINA
Charleston
SOUTH CAROLINA
Savannah
GEORGIA
St. Augustine
SPANISH FLORIDA
SPANISH LOUISIANA
St. Louis
Natchez
Baton Rouge
New Orleans
Mississippi R.
Gulf of Mexico
ATLANTIC OCEAN
BAHAMAS
CUBA
JAMAICA
Caribbean Sea
SANTO DOMINGO
STE. DOMINGUE
N
25°
30°
35°
40°
65°
75°
85°
20°

Scale:
0   150   300 mi
0   150   300 km

Though independent of British rule, the United States was not free from pressure from European nations. Hemmed in by British Canada to the north and Spanish claims to south and west, America struggled to establish its boundaries. Which boundary of the United States was most secure in 1783?

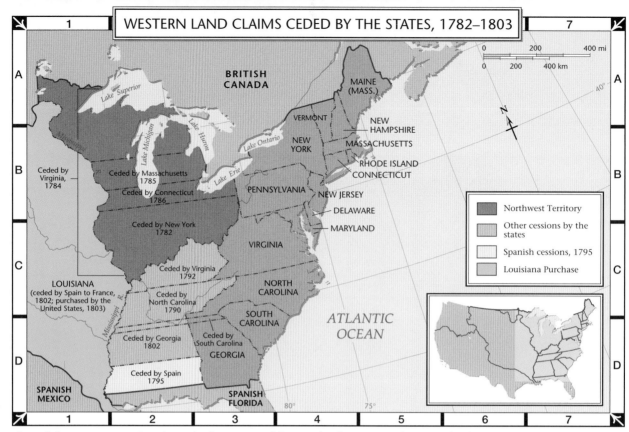

WESTERN LAND CLAIMS CEDED BY THE STATES, 1782–1803

Northwest Territory
Other cessions by the states
Spanish cessions, 1795
Louisiana Purchase

One of the most contentious issues in the new republic was the disposition of western lands. As American settlers started to move West, various states claimed territory that extended to the Mississippi River. After some maneuvering between politicians and land speculators, all the states ceded their lands to Congress. Then, in 1803, the nation doubled in size by the Louisiana Purchase. Why is the Native American presence not indicated on this map?

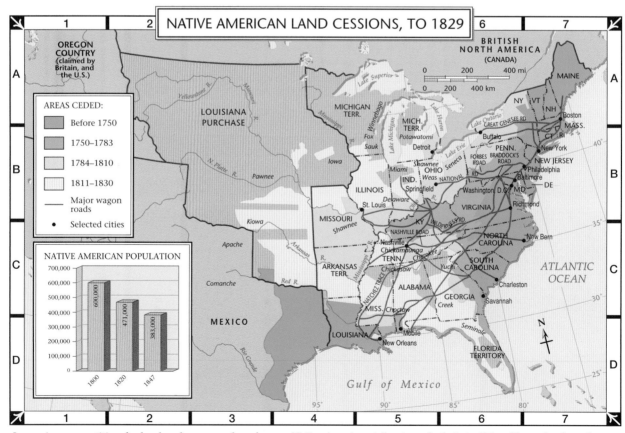

NATIVE AMERICAN LAND CESSIONS, TO 1829

AREAS CEDED:
Before 1750
1750–1783
1784–1810
1811–1830
Major wagon roads
Selected cities

NATIVE AMERICAN POPULATION

Increasing competition for land and resources forced many Native American tribes to cede their traditional homelands and move farther West. The depletion of game and other resources, along with epidemic diseases and warfare, also took their toll on Native American populations. How does the development of the road network correlate with the date of the land cessions?

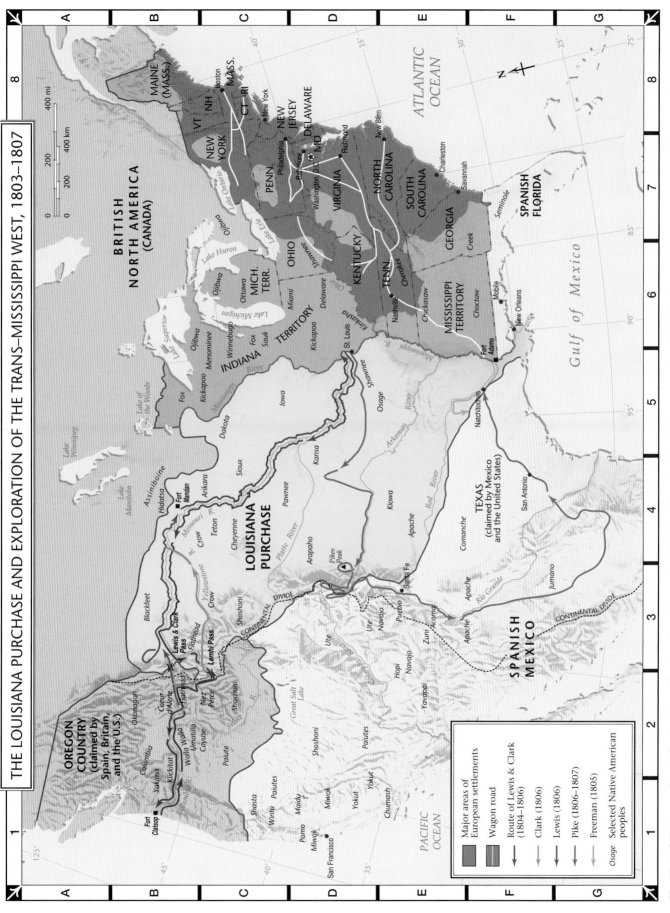

THE LOUISIANA PURCHASE AND EXPLORATION OF THE TRANS–MISSISSIPPI WEST, 1803–1807

The United States purchased the Louisiana Territory from France in 1803, doubling the size of the new nation. The federal government commissioned three expeditions to explore this region: Merriwether Lewis and William Clark's party headed up the Missouri River and traversed the northwest; Zebulon Pike and his men explored the southwest, entering Spanish territory in Mexico; and Thomas Freeman's group followed the Red River from the Mississippi river into Texas. Which geographical feature is suggested by the "islands" of sparse settlement in the Eastern United States?

19

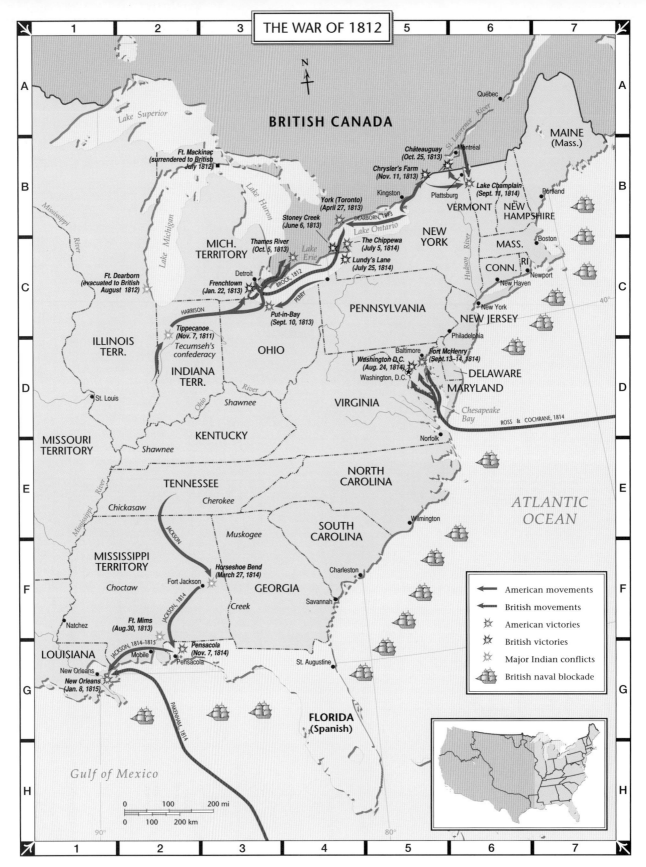

BRITISH CANADA

Québec

MAINE
(Mass.)

Châteauguay
(Oct. 25, 1813)

Montréal

Chrysler's Farm
(Nov. 11, 1813)

Kingston

Plattsburg

Lake Champlain
(Sept. 1u, 1814)

VERMONT

NEW
HAMPSHIRE

Portland

Ft. Mackinac
(surrendered to British
July 1812)

York (Toronto)
(April 27, 1813)

DEARBORN, 1813

Lake Ontario

NEW
YORK

MASS.

Boston

Stoney Creek
(June 6, 1813)

MICH.
TERRITORY

Thames River
(Oct. 5, 1813)

Lake Erie

The Chippewa
(July 5, 1814)

CONN.

RI

Newport

New Haven

Lundy's Lane
(July 25, 1814)

BROCK, 1812

PERRY

Ft. Dearborn
(evacuated to British
August 1812)

Detroit

Frenchtown
(Jan. 22, 1813)

PENNSYLVANIA

NEW YORK

New York

NEW JERSEY

40°

HARRISON

Put-in-Bay
(Sept. 10, 1813)

Philadelphia

ILLINOIS
TERR.

Tippecanoe
(Nov. 7, 1811)
Tecumseh's
confederacy

OHIO

Baltimore

Fort McHenry
(Sept.13–14, 1814)

Washington D.C.
(Aug. 24, 1814)

DELAWARE

INDIANA
TERR.

Ohio River

Washington, D.C.

MARYLAND

St. Louis

Shawnee

VIRGINIA

Chesapeake
Bay

ROSS & COCHRANE, 1814

MISSOURI
TERRITORY

KENTUCKY

Shawnee

Norfolk

Chickasaw

Cherokee

NORTH
CAROLINA

TENNESSEE

ATLANTIC
OCEAN

JACKSON

Muskogee

SOUTH
CAROLINA

Wilmington

MISSISSIPPI
TERRITORY

Choctaw

Fort Jackson

Horseshoe Bend
(March 27, 1814)

GEORGIA

Charleston

Creek

JACKSON, 1814

Savannah

Natchez

Ft. Mims
(Aug.30, 1813)

Pensacola
(Nov. 7, 1814)

JACKSON, 1814–1815

LOUISIANA

Mobile

Pensacola

St. Augustine

New Orleans

New Orleans
(Jan. 8, 1815)

PAKENHAM, 1814

FLORIDA
(Spanish)

Gulf of Mexico

←	American movements
←	British movements
✶	American victories
✶	British victories
✶	Major Indian conflicts
⛵	British naval blockade

Mississippi River

Lake Superior

Lake Michigan

Lake Huron

N

90°

80°

0   100   200 mi
0   100   200 km

The United States attempted to stay neutral in the European wars of the early nineteenth century. However, frustration with British interference with American shipping, coupled with the belief that England was supplying western Indian peoples with weapons, finally led to war. The fledgling nation was ill-equipped to take on a global power such as England, and suffered defeats in Canada, a British blockade of the coast, and the humiliation of having the nation's capital burned. A few weeks later, American forces held off a British attack at Fort McHenry, a victory memorialized in "The Star Spangled Banner." The American victory at Battle of New Orleans actually took place two weeks after the peace treaty had been signed. Why was so much of this war fought in coastal areas or along the Great Lakes?

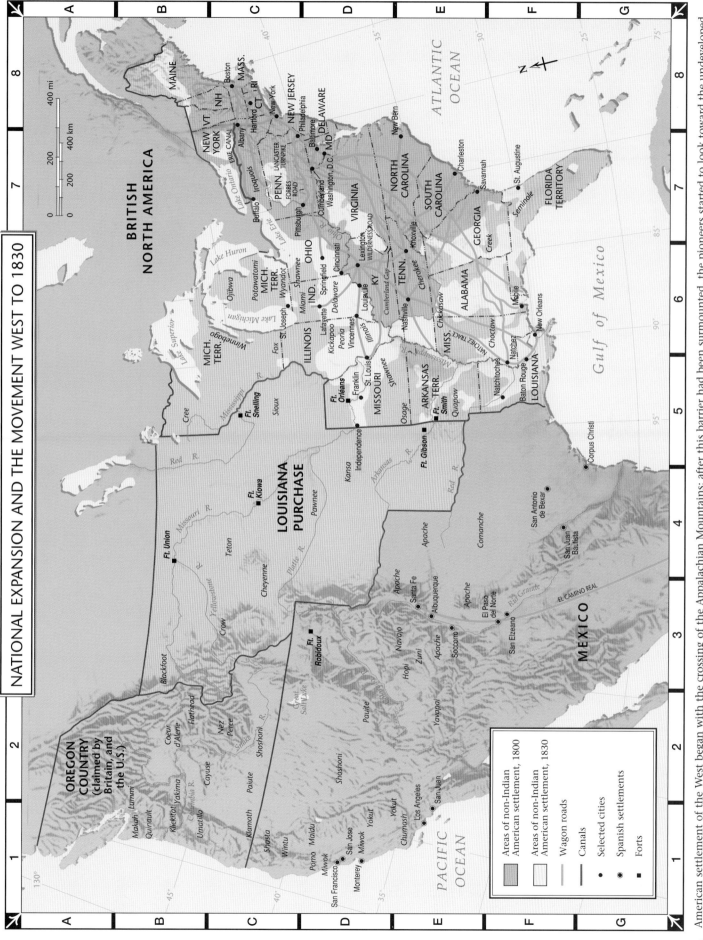

NATIONAL EXPANSION AND THE MOVEMENT WEST TO 1830

American settlement of the West began with the crossing of the Appalachian Mountains; after this barrier had been surmounted, the pioneers started to look toward the undeveloped land of the Louisiana Purchase. What role do rivers play in American settlement west of the Mississippi in 1830?

21

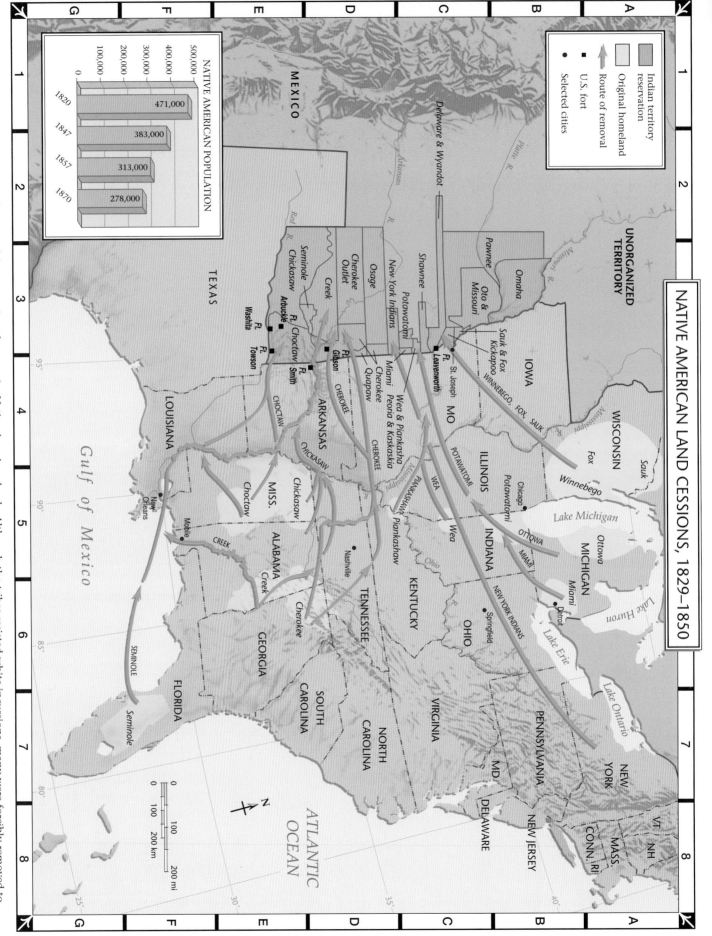

NATIVE AMERICAN LAND CESSIONS, 1829–1850

By treaty, warfare, and other methods, the United States continued to acquire Native American lands. Although the tribes resisted white incursions, many were forcibly removed to reservations in the west. Why were the Missouri River and the 95th meridian used for the boundary of so many reservations?

NATIVE AMERICAN POPULATION

Year	Population
1820	471,000
1847	383,000
1857	313,000
1870	278,000

Legend:
- Indian territory reservation
- Original homeland
- Route of removal
- U.S. fort
- Selected cities

MISSOURI COMPROMISE OF 1820–1821

Map legend:
- Free states and territories
- Territory in which slavery was prohibited by the Missouri Compromise
- Slave states and territories
- Territory in which slavery was not permitted by the Missouri Compromise
- Areas of major European settlement

Slavery increasingly divided Americans along sectional lines. The contentious issue of expanding slavery to the new territories was temporarily resolved by the compromise of 1820-1821, in which Missouri was admitted as a slave state and Maine as a free state, thus preserving an even balance in the U.S. Senate. Territory south of the compromise line of 36° 30′ was declared open to slavery; to the north, slavery was prohibited. If the territorial expansion of the United States had stopped in 1821, would the Missouri Compromise have favored the North or the South?

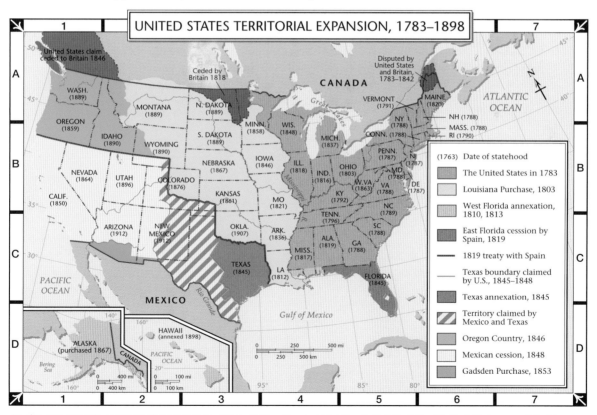

UNITED STATES TERRITORIAL EXPANSION, 1783–1898

Map legend:
- (1763) Date of statehood
- The United States in 1783
- Louisiana Purchase, 1803
- West Florida annexation, 1810, 1813
- East Florida cesssion by Spain, 1819
- 1819 treaty with Spain
- Texas boundary claimed by U.S., 1845–1848
- Texas annexation, 1845
- Territory claimed by Mexico and Texas
- Oregon Country, 1846
- Mexican cession, 1848
- Gadsden Purchase, 1853

In the nineteenth century, the term "manifest destiny" expressed the belief that the United States was fated to extend across the continent. Toward that end, America had acquired Florida from Spain; purchased the Louisiana territory from France; established its northern boundary and gained Oregon from Great Britain; and taken much of the southwest from Mexico through war and purchase. By the end of the century, the nation had extended even further by purchasing Alaska from Russia, annexing the Hawaiian Islands and acquiring Spanish territories in the Caribbean and the Philippines. The United States shares a common boundary with only two other nations. Why is this significant?

23

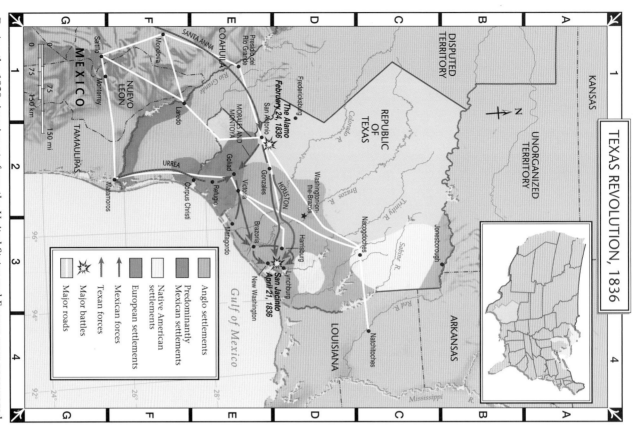

TEXAS REVOLUTION, 1836

During the 1820s immigrants from the United States and Europe were encouraged to settle in Texas, then the northernmost state of Mexico. In the 1830s, frustrated by government restrictions and concerned about the political rise of the Mexican dictator Santa Anna, the Texans revolted. Although one group, comprised of both Anglos and Tejanos suffered defeat at the Alamo, the Texans finally crushed Mexican forces led by Santa Anna at San Jacinto in 1836. Texas became an independent republic until 1845, when it became the twenty-eighth state. Note that most of Texas is drained by its own rivers, rather than by the Rio Grande or the Mississippi. How would this encourage an independent spirit?

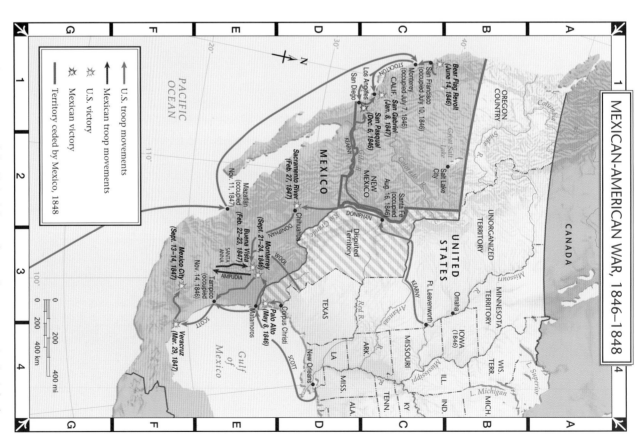

MEXICAN-AMERICAN WAR, 1846–1848

War with Mexico gained the United States the southwestern territories it had long coveted. Invading American armies won a series of victories and entered Mexico City in 1847. Other troops were dispatched across the mountains and deserts of the interior to assist American settlers in California who had revolted against the Mexican government. How did the fleet commanded by Stockton reach California?

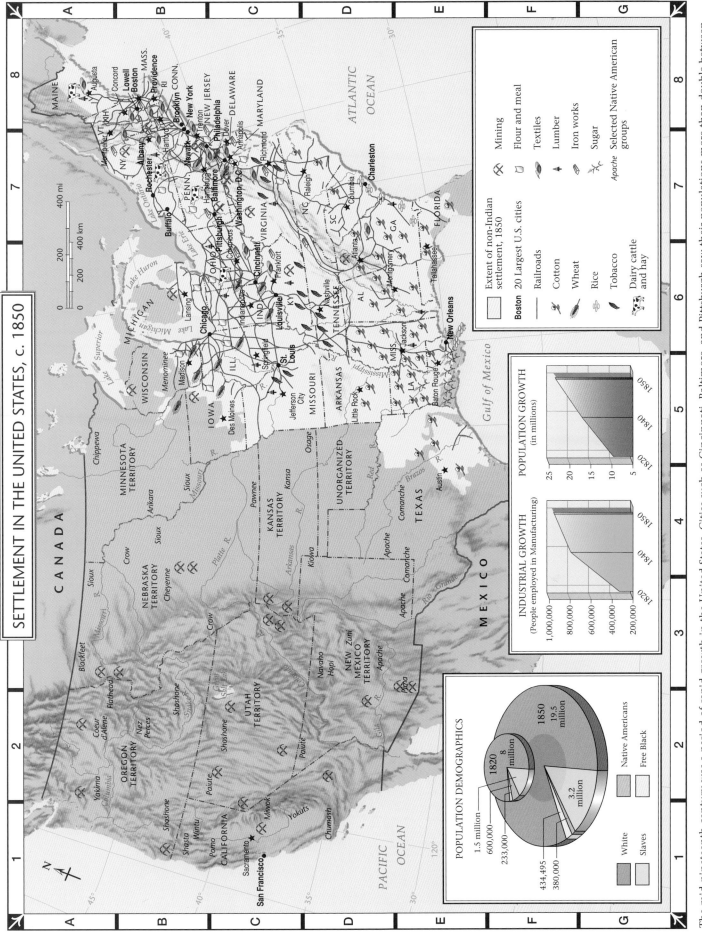

SETTLEMENT IN THE UNITED STATES, c. 1850

POPULATION GROWTH
(in millions)

INDUSTRIAL GROWTH
(People employed in Manufacturing)

POPULATION DEMOGRAPHICS

1.5 million
600,000
233,000

1820
8 million

1850
19.5 million

3.2 million

434,495
380,000

White
Slaves
Native Americans
Free Black

LEGEND

Extent of non-Indian settlement, 1850

Boston 20 Largest U.S. cities

Railroads

Cotton

Wheat

Rice

Tobacco

Dairy cattle and hay

Mining

Flour and meal

Textiles

Lumber

Iron works

Sugar

Apache Selected Native American groups

The mid-nineteenth century was a period of rapid growth in the United States. Cities such as Cincinnati, Baltimore, and Pittsburgh saw their populations more than double between 1840 and 1850. Cities in the western states showed the most remarkable growth: St. Louis nearly quadrupled in size, and Chicago's population increased sevenfold. Population gains were more modest in the South, where cotton continued to dominate the economy. Which state had the most diverse economy about 1850?

25

GROWTH OF THE TRANSPORTATION SYSTEM, 1840–1860

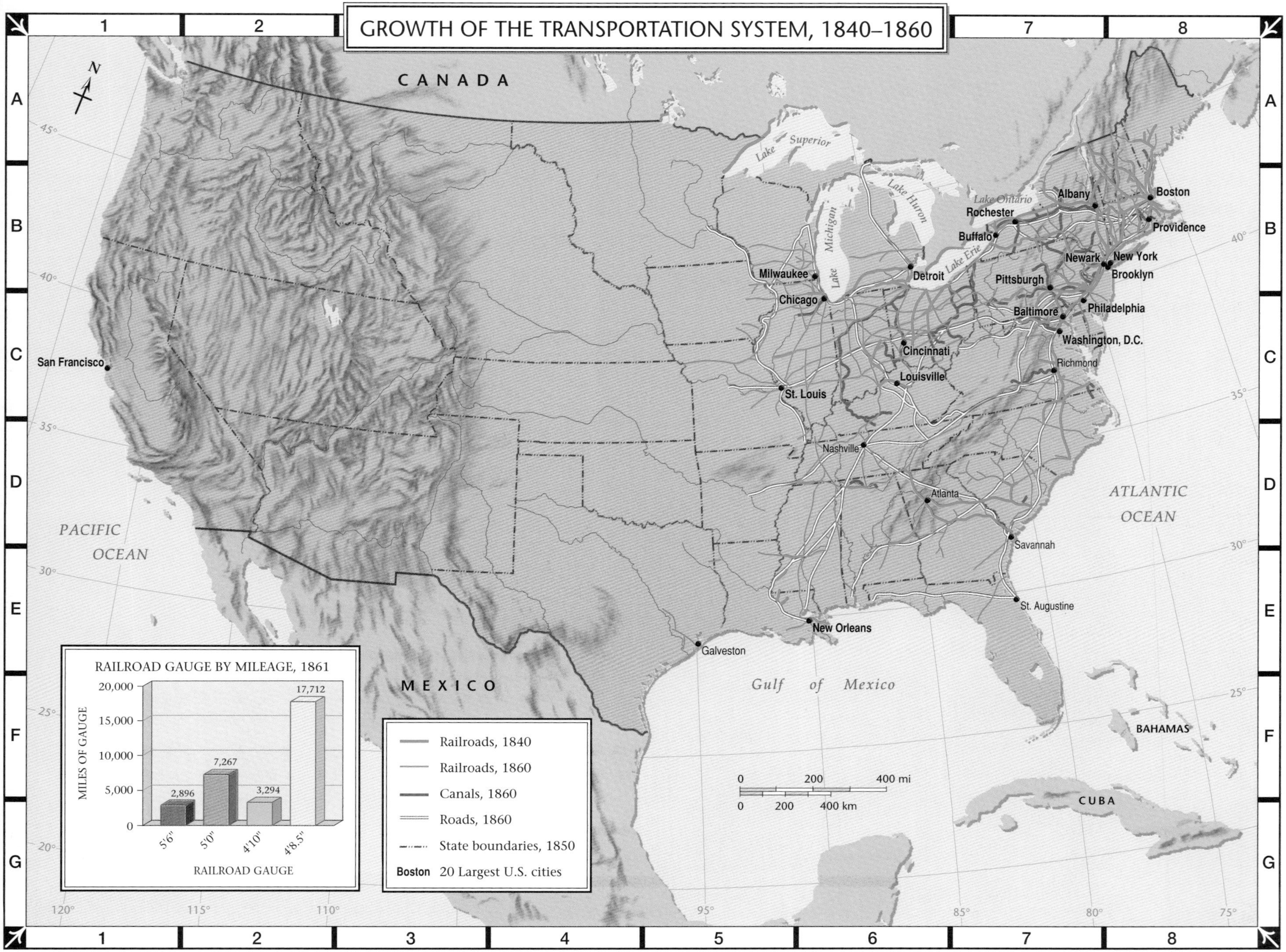

RAILROAD GAUGE BY MILEAGE, 1861

MILES OF GAUGE

RAILROAD GAUGE

Gauge	Mileage
5'6"	2,896
5'0"	7,267
4'10"	3,294
4'8.5"	17,712

Railroads, 1840
Railroads, 1860
Canals, 1860
Roads, 1860
State boundaries, 1850
Boston 20 Largest U.S. cities

PACIFIC OCEAN

CANADA

MEXICO

Gulf of Mexico

ATLANTIC OCEAN

CUBA

BAHAMAS

San Francisco
Galveston
New Orleans
St. Louis
Nashville
Atlanta
Louisville
Cincinnati
Chicago
Milwaukee
Detroit
Buffalo
Rochester
Pittsburgh
Baltimore
Richmond
Washington, D.C.
Philadelphia
Newark
Brooklyn
New York
Albany
Providence
Boston
Savannah
St. Augustine

Lake Superior
Lake Michigan
Lake Huron
Lake Erie
Lake Ontario

0 200 400 km
0 200 400 mi

Railroads proved a valuable addition to America's system of roads and canals, particularly in the North. However, construction was largely unregulated; as a result, there was no standard track gauge, and by the time of the Civil War, there were at least seven different gauges in operation. What accounts for the difference in railroad development north and south of the Ohio Rivers in 1860?

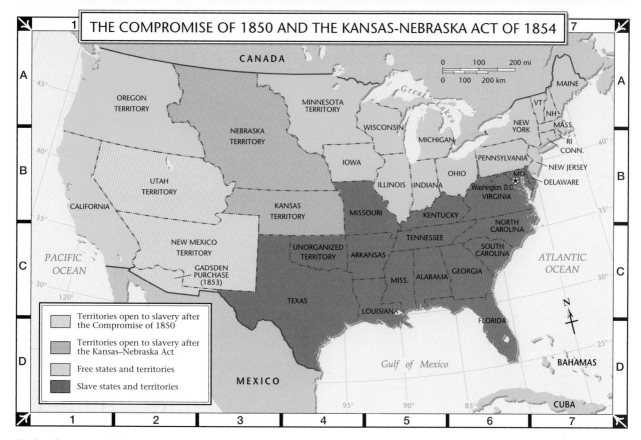

THE COMPROMISE OF 1850 AND THE KANSAS-NEBRASKA ACT OF 1854

Legend:
- Territories open to slavery after the Compromise of 1850
- Territories open to slavery after the Kansas–Nebraska Act
- Free states and territories
- Slave states and territories

Under the terms of the Compromise of 1850, slavery was prohibited in the remaining lands from the Louisiana Purchase; however, four years later this same area was opened to slavery by the Kansas-Nebraska Act. The agreement also permitted the continuation of slavery in Washington, D.C., but abolished the slave trade there. Would the pattern of political compromise in the decades following 1820 have been different if Missouri had been admitted as a free state?

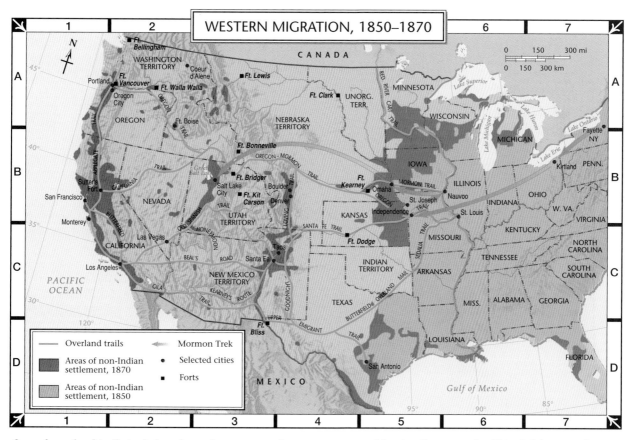

WESTERN MIGRATION, 1850–1870

Legend:
- Overland trails
- Mormon Trek
- Areas of non-Indian settlement, 1870
- Areas of non-Indian settlement, 1850
- Selected cities
- Forts

Several overland trails took American pioneers west. Some were attracted by the discovery of gold in California; others sought new farmlands in the fertile Oregon country. The Mormons fled religious persecution in the East to form a community in Utah. Why did no major trail follow the route established by Lewis and Clark?

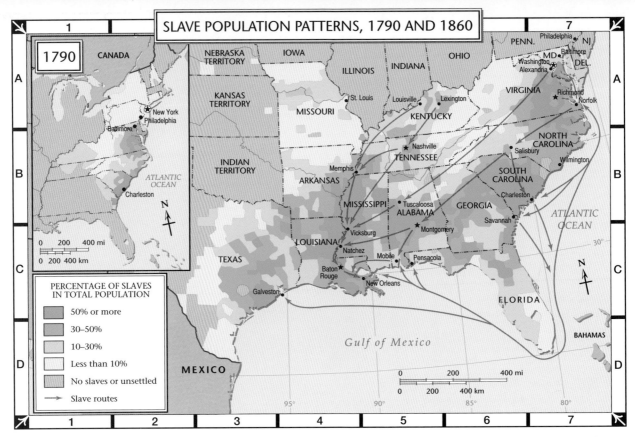

SLAVE POPULATION PATTERNS, 1790 AND 1860

1790

PERCENTAGE OF SLAVES IN TOTAL POPULATION

- 50% or more
- 30–50%
- 10–30%
- Less than 10%
- No slaves or unsettled
- → Slave routes

Although the importation of slaves to the United States was outlawed in 1808, a profitable internal trade developed to supply the needs of new plantations. As cotton grew in importance as an export crop, and as the nation's boundaries expanded, more land came under cultivation in the Deep South and East Texas. Why were slaves concentrated in the lands adjacent to the Mississippi river?

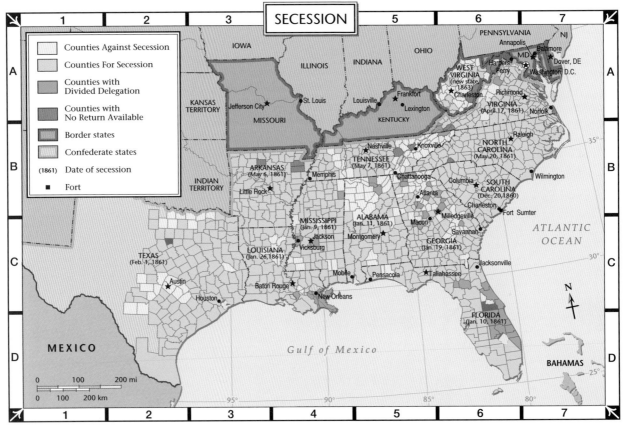

SECESSION

- Counties Against Secession
- Counties For Secession
- Counties with Divided Delegation
- Counties with No Return Available
- Border states
- Confederate states
- (1861) Date of secession
- ■ Fort

The South Carolina legislature voted to withdraw from the Union immediately following the election of Abraham Lincoln. By May, ten other southern states had joined them to form the Confederate States of America. Four slaveholding states—Missouri, Kentucky, Maryland, and Delaware—became "border" states. Divided opinion in Virginia led to the separation of West Virginia, which was admitted to the Union as a border state in 1863. Which states in the Confederacy had counties which voted against secession?

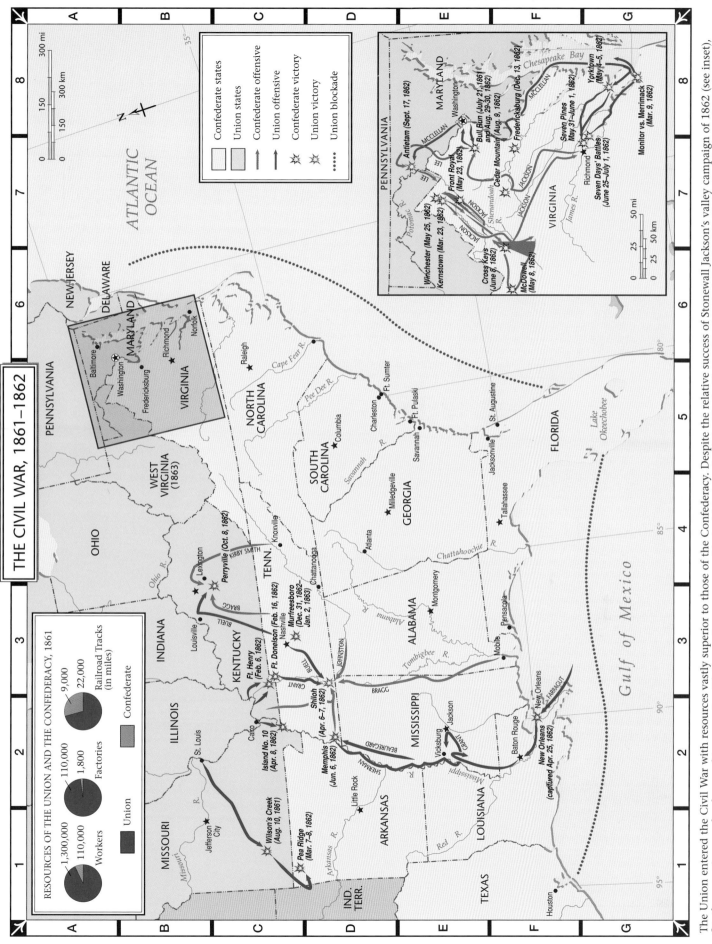

THE CIVIL WAR, 1861–1862

RESOURCES OF THE UNION AND THE CONFEDERACY, 1861

- 1,300,000 / 110,000 — Workers
- 110,000 / 18,00 — Factories
- 22,000 / 9,000 — Railroad Tracks (in miles)

- Union
- Confederate

Legend:
- Confederate states
- Union states
- Confederate offensive
- Union offensive
- Confederate victory
- Union victory
- Union blockade

Inset map battles:
- Antietam (Sept. 17, 1862)
- Bull Run (July 21, 1861 and Aug. 29–30, 1862)
- Fredericksburg (Dec. 13, 1862)
- Yorktown (May 4–5, 1862)
- Monitor vs. Merrimack (Mar. 9, 1862)
- Seven Pines May 31–June 1, 1862
- Seven Days' Battles (June 25–July 1, 1862)
- Cedar Mountain (Aug. 9, 1862)
- Front Royal (May 23, 1862)
- Winchester (May 25, 1862)
- Kernstown (Mar. 23, 1862)
- Cross Keys (June 8, 1862)
- McDowell (May 8, 1862)
- Richmond

Main map battles:
- Perryville (Oct. 8, 1862)
- Ft. Henry (Feb. 6, 1862)
- Ft. Donelson (Feb. 16, 1862)
- Murfreesboro (Dec. 31, 1862, Jan. 2, 1863)
- Shiloh (Apr. 6–7, 1862)
- Island No. 10 (Apr. 8, 1862)
- Memphis (Jun. 6, 1862)
- Wilson's Creek (Aug. 10, 1861)
- Pea Ridge (Mar. 7–8, 1862)
- New Orleans (captured Apr. 25, 1862)

The Union entered the Civil War with resources vastly superior to those of the Confederacy. Despite the relative success of Stonewall Jackson's valley campaign of 1862 (see inset), Southern armies were hard-pressed to compete with the vast manpower and industrial strength of the North. The national capital remained in Union hands throughout the war even though it was surrounded by slaveholding states. Why didn't the Confederacy attack Washington, D.C.?

29

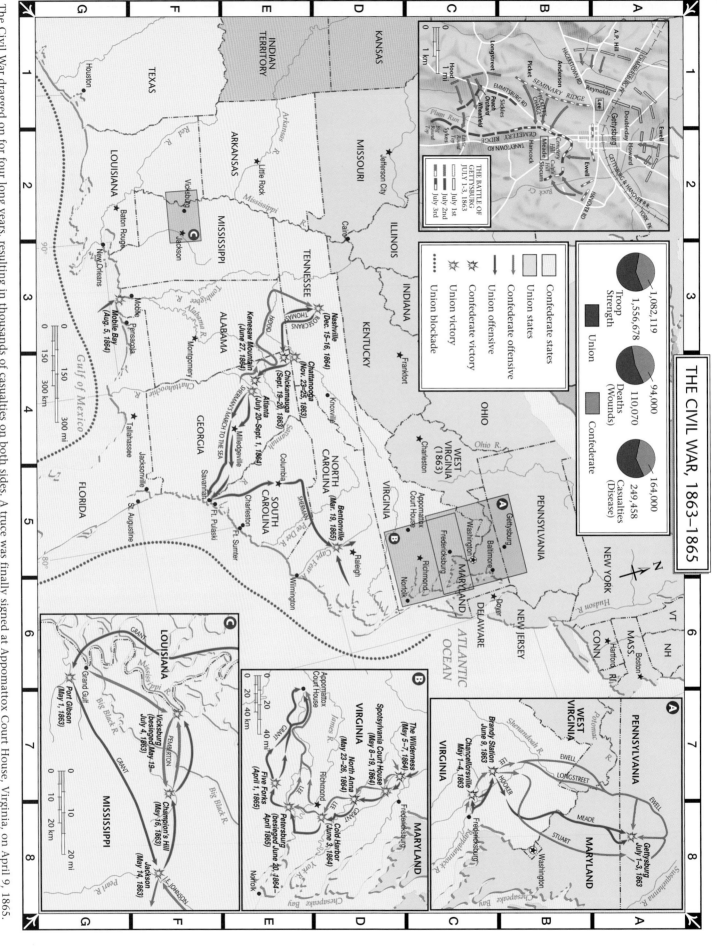

THE CIVIL WAR, 1863–1865

The Civil War dragged on for four long years, resulting in thousands of casualties on both sides. A truce was finally signed at Appomattox Court House, Virginia, on April 9, 1865. The inset maps provide greater detail on important campaigns. How are these campaigns connected in the general flow of military action?

THE BATTLE OF GETTYSBURG
JULY 1-3, 1863

- July 1st
- July 2nd
- July 3rd

Troop Strength
- 1,082,119
- 1,556,678

Deaths (Wounds)
- 94,000
- 110,070

Casualties (Disease)
- 164,000
- 249,458

- Union
- Confederate

Legend
- Confederate states
- Union states
- Confederate offensive
- Union offensive
- Confederate victory
- Union victory
- Union blockade

INSET A

PENNSYLVANIA
WEST VIRGINIA
VIRGINIA
MARYLAND
Brandy Station June 9, 1863
Chancellorsville May 1-4, 1863
Gettysburg July 1-3, 1863
Fredericksburg
Washington
Shenandoah R.
Rappahannock R.
Potomac R.
EWELL, LONGSTREET, MEADE, HOOKER, STUART, LEE

INSET B

VIRGINIA
MARYLAND
Appomattox Court House
Spotsylvania Court House (May 8-19, 1864)
The Wilderness (May 5-7, 1864)
North Anna (May 23-26, 1864)
Five Forks (April 1, 1865)
Cold Harbor (June 3, 1864)
Petersburg (besieged June 20, 1864 - April 1865)
Richmond
Fredericksburg
Norfolk
James R.
York R.
Chesapeake Bay
GRANT, LEE
0 20 40 mi
0 20 40 km

INSET C

LOUISIANA
MISSISSIPPI
Grand Gulf
Port Gibson (May 1, 1863)
Vicksburg (besieged May 19 - July 4, 1863)
Champion's Hill (May 16, 1863)
Jackson (May 14, 1863)
Mississippi R.
Big Black R.
Pearl R.
GRANT, PEMBERTON, J.E. JOHNSON
0 10 20 mi
0 10 20 km

Main Map Labels

TEXAS
Houston
LOUISIANA
Baton Rouge
New Orleans
ARKANSAS
Little Rock
Jefferson City
MISSOURI
Cairo
ILLINOIS
INDIANA
KANSAS
INDIAN TERRITORY
MISSISSIPPI
Vicksburg
Jackson
Mobile Bay (Aug. 5, 1864)
Mobile
Pensacola
Montgomery
Tallahassee
ALABAMA
GEORGIA
Kenesaw Mountain (June 27, 1864)
Chickamauga (Sept. 19-20, 1863)
Chattanooga (Nov. 23-25, 1863)
Atlanta (July 20-Sept. 1, 1864)
Milledgeville
Savannah
Ft. Pulaski
TENNESSEE
Nashville (Dec. 15-16, 1864)
Knoxville
KENTUCKY
Frankfort
OHIO
Charleston
WEST VIRGINIA (1863)
VIRGINIA
Appomattox Court House
Richmond
Norfolk
Fredericksburg
Washington
Baltimore
Gettysburg
MARYLAND
DELAWARE
Dover
PENNSYLVANIA
NEW JERSEY
NEW YORK
CONN.
Hartford
Boston
MASS.
R.I.
NH
VT
NORTH CAROLINA
Bentonville (Mar. 19, 1865)
Raleigh
Wilmington
SOUTH CAROLINA
Columbia
Charleston
Ft. Sumter
FLORIDA
Jacksonville
St. Augustine
Gulf of Mexico
ATLANTIC OCEAN
SHERMAN'S MARCH TO THE SEA
ROSECRANS, THOMAS, HOOD, SHERMAN
Mississippi R., Red R., Arkansas R., Ohio R., Hudson R., Susquehanna R., Alabama R., Chattahoochee R., Tombigbee R., Cape Fear R., Pee Dee R.

0 150 300 mi
0 150 300 km

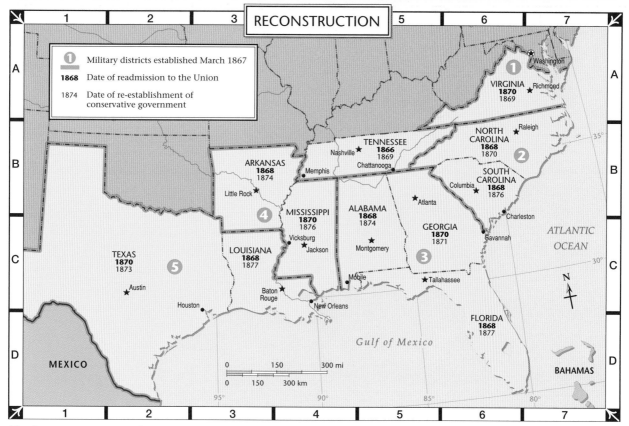

RECONSTRUCTION

① Military districts established March 1867

1868 Date of readmission to the Union

1874 Date of re-establishment of conservative government

VIRGINIA **1870** 1869 — Richmond — Washington

TENNESSEE **1866** 1869 — Nashville — Chattanooga

NORTH CAROLINA **1868** 1870 — Raleigh ②

ARKANSAS **1868** 1874 — Memphis — Little Rock ④

SOUTH CAROLINA **1868** 1876 — Columbia — Charleston

MISSISSIPPI **1870** 1876 — Vicksburg — Jackson

ALABAMA **1868** 1874 — Atlanta

GEORGIA **1870** 1871 ③ — Savannah

ATLANTIC OCEAN

TEXAS **1870** 1873 ⑤ — Austin

LOUISIANA **1868** 1877 — Baton Rouge — New Orleans — Houston

Montgomery — Mobile — Tallahassee

FLORIDA **1868** 1877

MEXICO

0   150   300 mi
0   150   300 km

Gulf of Mexico

BAHAMAS

The Reconstruction Act of 1867 divided the ten southern states (Tennessee had already been readmitted to the Union) into five military districts. During this period, southern state governments were first controlled by white ex-Confederates, then by white opponents of the Confederacy and African Americans, and finally "redeemed" by conservative white Democrats. Which states were the last ones in which conservative Democrats regained control?

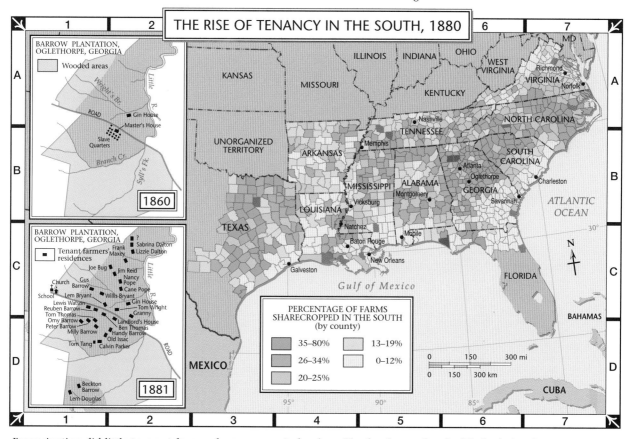

THE RISE OF TENANCY IN THE SOUTH, 1880

BARROW PLANTATION, OGLETHORPE, GEORGIA

Wooded areas

Wright's Br. — Little R. — ROAD — Gin House — Master's House — Slave Quarters — Branch Cr. — Sull's Fk.

1860

BARROW PLANTATION, OGLETHORPE, GEORGIA

■ Tenant farmers' residences

Frank Maxey — Sabrina Dalton — Lizzie Dalton — ? — Joe Bug — Jim Reid — Nancy Pope — Cane Pope — Church — Gus Barrow — School — Lem Bryant — Willis Bryant — Gin House — Lewis Watson — Tom Wright — Reuben Barrow — Granny — Tom Thomas — Landlord's House — Omy Barrow — Ben Thomas — Peter Barrow — Handy Barrow — Milly Barrow — Old Issac — Tom Tang — Calvin Parker — Little R. — ROAD — Beckton Barrow — Lem Douglas

1881

KANSAS — MISSOURI — ILLINOIS — INDIANA — OHIO — WEST VIRGINIA — MD — VIRGINIA — Richmond — Norfolk

KENTUCKY — UNORGANIZED TERRITORY — ARKANSAS — Memphis — Nashville — TENNESSEE — NORTH CAROLINA

MISSISSIPPI — ALABAMA — Atlanta — Oglethorpe — GEORGIA — SOUTH CAROLINA — Charleston — Montgomery — Savannah

TEXAS — LOUISIANA — Vicksburg — Natchez — Baton Rouge — Mobile — New Orleans — ATLANTIC OCEAN

Galveston — FLORIDA

MEXICO — Gulf of Mexico — BAHAMAS — CUBA

PERCENTAGE OF FARMS SHARECROPPED IN THE SOUTH (by county)

35–80%   13–19%
26–34%   0–12%
20–25%

0   150   300 mi
0   150   300 km

Emancipation did little to grant former slaves economic freedom. The freedmen often had little choice than to continue to work for their former masters as tenant farmers, or sharecroppers. In addition, the depressed economy of the 1870s forced many poor white farmers into tenancy. Forced to cultivate a single cash crop such as cotton, both white and black sharecroppers were vulnerable to market fluctuations which could leave them deeply in debt and render them virtual serfs of the landowner. Why might farm tenancy have been less common along in some coastal regions?

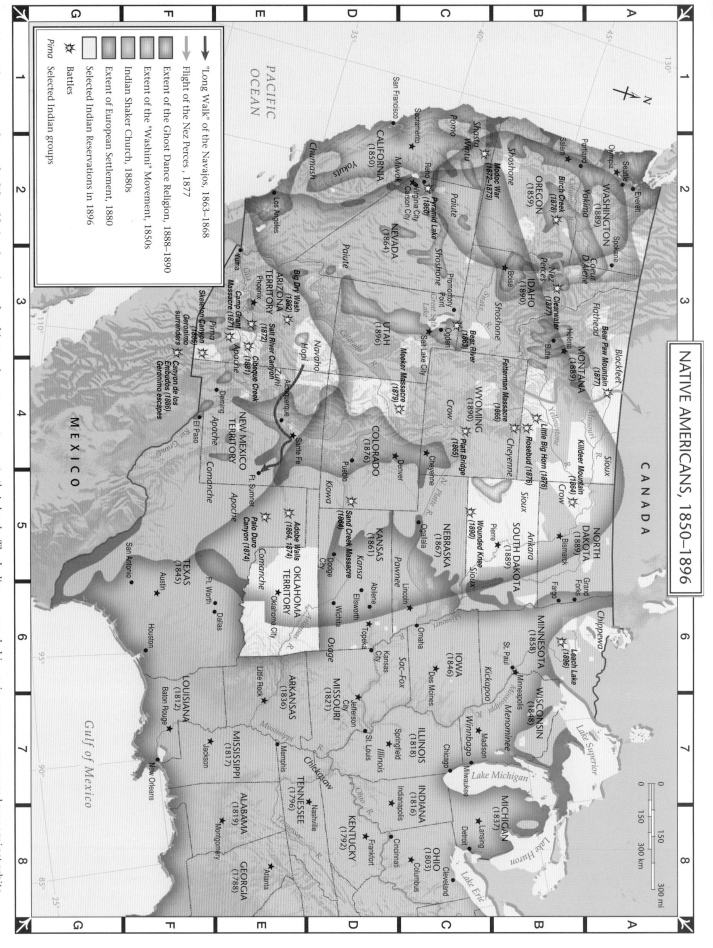

NATIVE AMERICANS, 1850–1896

As white settlers streamed into the West, Native Americans faced increasing pressure to vacate their lands. The Indians responded in various ways: some waged war against white Americans; others moved to government-sponsored reservations; while many others sought strength and solace in new religious movements. The 100th meridian is often described as the boundary between wet America and dry America. What does this suggest about the division of land in South Dakota in 1896?

32

Legend

"Long Walk" of the Navajos, 1863–1868

Flight of the Nez Perces, 1877

Extent of the Ghost Dance Religion, 1888–1890

Extent of the "Washini" Movement, 1850s

Indian Shaker Church, 1880s

Extent of European Settlement, 1880

Selected Indian Reservations in 1896

Battles

Pima Selected Indian groups

Map labels

PACIFIC OCEAN

CANADA

MEXICO

Gulf of Mexico

Lake Superior
Lake Michigan
Lake Huron
Lake Erie

WASHINGTON (1889)
OREGON (1859)
CALIFORNIA (1850)
NEVADA (1864)
IDAHO (1890)
MONTANA (1889)
UTAH (1896)
WYOMING (1890)
ARIZONA TERRITORY
NEW MEXICO TERRITORY
COLORADO (1876)
NORTH DAKOTA (1889)
SOUTH DAKOTA (1889)
NEBRASKA (1867)
KANSAS (1861)
OKLAHOMA TERRITORY
TEXAS (1845)
MINNESOTA (1858)
IOWA (1846)
MISSOURI (1821)
ARKANSAS (1836)
LOUISIANA (1812)
WISCONSIN (1848)
ILLINOIS (1818)
MICHIGAN (1837)
INDIANA (1816)
KENTUCKY (1792)
TENNESSEE (1796)
MISSISSIPPI (1817)
ALABAMA (1819)
GEORGIA (1788)
OHIO (1803)

Cities: San Francisco, Sacramento, Los Angeles, Salem, Portland, Seattle, Olympia, Everett, Spokane, Yakima, Reno, Virginia City, Carson City, Boise, Helena, Butte, Phoenix, Yuma, Deming, El Paso, Santa Fe, Albuquerque, Salt Lake City, Ogden, Promontory Point, Cheyenne, Denver, Pueblo, Pierre, Oglala, Bismarck, Grand Forks, Fargo, Lincoln, Omaha, Topeka, Kansas City, Dodge City, Abilene, Ellsworth, Wichita, St. Paul, Minneapolis, Madison, Milwaukee, Chicago, Des Moines, Jefferson City, St. Louis, Springfield, Indianapolis, Cincinnati, Columbus, Cleveland, Detroit, Lansing, Frankfort, Nashville, Memphis, Little Rock, Jackson, Baton Rouge, New Orleans, Houston, Dallas, Ft. Worth, Austin, San Antonio, Oklahoma City, Montgomery, Atlanta

Native groups: Pomo, Shasta, Wintu, Miwok, Yokuts, Chumash, Paiute, Shoshone, Nez Perces, Flathead, Coeur D'Alene, Blackfeet, Crow, Sioux, Arikara, Cheyenne, Hopi, Navaho, Zuni, Apache, Comanche, Kiowa, Osage, Pawnee, Kansa, Sac-Fox, Kickapoo, Menominee, Winnebago, Chippewa, Chickasaw

Rivers/features: Columbia R., Snake R., Great Salt Lake, Colorado R., Gila R., Rio Grande, Missouri R., Yellowstone R., N. Platte R., S. Platte R., Arkansas R., Mississippi R., Ohio R., Tennessee R.

Battles and events:
Modoc War (1872–1873)
Birch Creek (1878)
Pyramid Lake (1860)
Big Dry Wash (1882)
Camp Grant Massacre (1871)
Salt River Canyon (1872)
Skeleton Canyon (1886) Geronimo surrenders
Canyon de los Embudos (1886) Geronimo escapes
Cibeque Creek (1881)
Clearwater (1877)
Bear Paw Mountain (1877)
Killdeer Mountain (1864)
Little Big Horn (1876)
Rosebud (1876)
Fetterman Massacre (1866)
Platt Bridge (1865)
Meeker Massacre (1879)
Wounded Knee (1890)
Leach Lake (1896)
Sand Creek Massacre (1864)
Adobe Walls (1864, 1874)
Palo Duro Canyon (1874)
Ft. Sumner

Compass: N

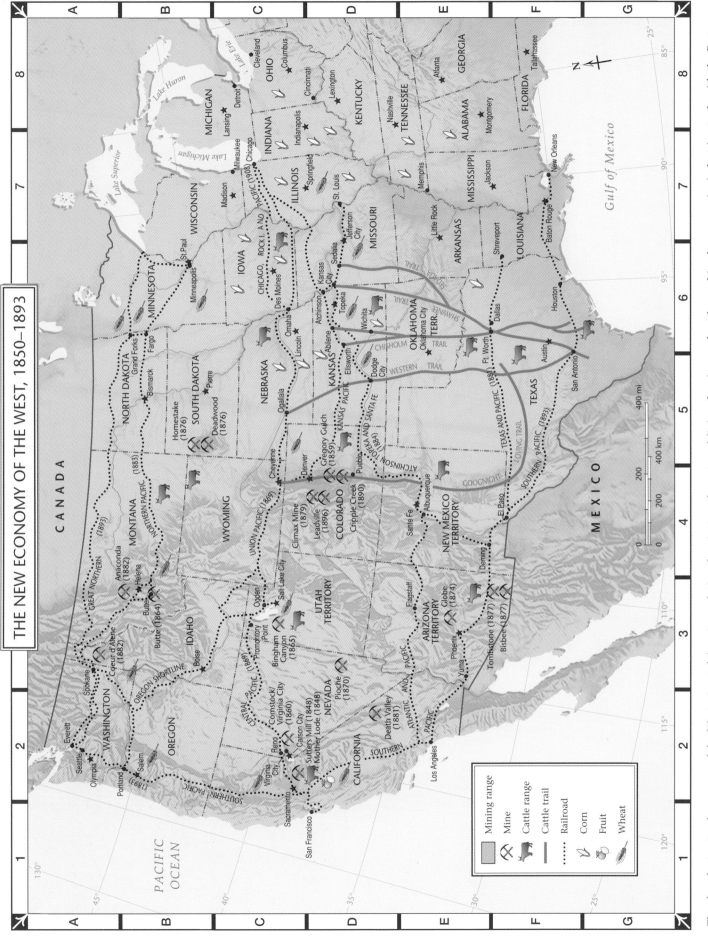

THE NEW ECONOMY OF THE WEST, 1850–1893

Legend:
- Mining range
- Mine
- Cattle range
- Cattle trail
- Railroad
- Corn
- Fruit
- Wheat

CANADA

MEXICO

PACIFIC OCEAN

Gulf of Mexico

States and Territories:
WASHINGTON, OREGON, IDAHO, MONTANA, WYOMING, NORTH DAKOTA, SOUTH DAKOTA, MINNESOTA, WISCONSIN, MICHIGAN, IOWA, NEBRASKA, NEVADA, CALIFORNIA, UTAH TERRITORY, COLORADO, KANSAS, MISSOURI, ILLINOIS, INDIANA, OHIO, KENTUCKY, TENNESSEE, ARIZONA TERRITORY, NEW MEXICO TERRITORY, OKLAHOMA TERR., TEXAS, ARKANSAS, LOUISIANA, MISSISSIPPI, ALABAMA, GEORGIA, FLORIDA

Railroads:
GREAT NORTHERN (1893), NORTHERN PACIFIC (1883), OREGON SHORTLINE (1884), CENTRAL PACIFIC (1869), UNION PACIFIC (1869), SOUTHERN PACIFIC, ATLANTIC AND PACIFIC, SOUTHERN PACIFIC (1883), KANSAS PACIFIC, ATCHISON TOPEKA AND SANTA FE, CHICAGO, ROCK ISLAND AND PACIFIC (1908), TEXAS AND PACIFIC (1884)

Cattle trails:
SEDALIA TRAIL, SHAWNEE TRAIL, CHISHOLM TRAIL, WESTERN TRAIL, GOODNIGHT-LOVING TRAIL

Mines and dates:
Coeur d'Alene (1882), Anaconda (1882), Butte (1864), Homestake (1876), Deadwood (1876), Comstock/Virginia City (1860), Sutter's Mill (1848), Mother Lode (1848), Carson City, Pioche (1870), Death Valley (1881), Bingham Canyon (1865), Gregory Gulch (1859), Climax Mine (1879), Leadville (1896), Cripple Creek (1890), Globe (1874), Tombstone (1877), Bisbee (1877), Promontory Point (1869)

Cities:
Seattle, Olympia, Everett, Spokane, Portland (1893), Salem, Boise, Helena, Butte, Grand Forks, Bismarck, Fargo, Pierre, St. Paul, Minneapolis, Madison, Milwaukee, Chicago, Detroit, Lansing, Cleveland, Columbus, Cincinnati, Indianapolis, Springfield, St. Louis, Jefferson City, Sedalia, Topeka, Atchison, Kansas City, Wichita, Abilene, Ellsworth, Dodge City, Des Moines, Omaha, Lincoln, Ogallala, Salt Lake City, Ogden, Cheyenne, Denver, Pueblo, Santa Fe, Albuquerque, El Paso, Deming, Flagstaff, Phoenix, Yuma, Los Angeles, San Francisco, Sacramento, Reno, Virginia City, Carson City, Oklahoma City, Ft. Worth, Dallas, Austin, San Antonio, Houston, Shreveport, Baton Rouge, New Orleans, Little Rock, Memphis, Jackson, Nashville, Lexington, Montgomery, Atlanta, Tallahassee

Lake Superior, Lake Michigan, Lake Huron, Lake Erie

Scale: 400 mi / 400 km / 200 / 0

The abundant natural resources of the West attracted Americans during the nineteenth century. Mining, farming, and cattle ranching became major industries; trade with the East was facilitated by the growth of the railroads. Why did these railroads have an east-west orientation rather than following a north-south route?

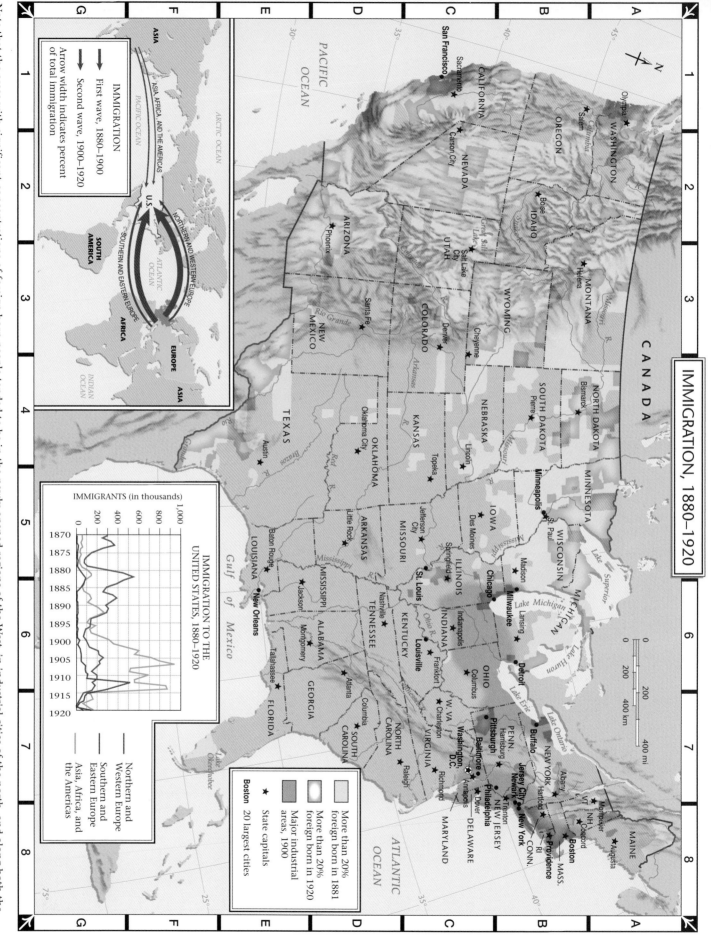

IMMIGRATION, 1880–1920

IMMIGRATION

First wave, 1880–1900

Second wave, 1900–1920

Arrow width indicates percent of total immigration

ASIA, AFRICA, AND THE AMERICAS

NORTHERN AND WESTERN EUROPE

SOUTHERN AND EASTERN EUROPE

ASIA
SOUTH AMERICA
AFRICA
EUROPE
ASIA

PACIFIC OCEAN
ARCTIC OCEAN
ATLANTIC OCEAN
INDIAN OCEAN

U.S.

IMMIGRATION TO THE UNITED STATES, 1880–1920

IMMIGRANTS (in thousands)

1,000 800 600 400 200 0

1870
1875
1880
1885
1890
1895
1900
1905
1910
1915
1920

Northern and Western Europe

Southern and Eastern Europe

Asia, Africa, and the Americas

More than 20% foreign born in 1881

More than 20% foreign born in 1920

Major industrial areas, 1900

★ State capitals

● **Boston** 20 largest cities

PACIFIC OCEAN
ATLANTIC OCEAN
Gulf of Mexico

CANADA

WASHINGTON — Olympia ★, Salem ★
OREGON
CALIFORNIA — San Francisco ●, Sacramento ★, Carson City ★
NEVADA
IDAHO — Boise ★
MONTANA — Helena ★
WYOMING — Cheyenne ★
UTAH — Salt Lake City ★
ARIZONA — Phoenix ★
COLORADO — Denver ★
NEW MEXICO — Santa Fe ★
NORTH DAKOTA — Bismarck ★
SOUTH DAKOTA — Pierre ★
NEBRASKA — Lincoln ★
KANSAS — Topeka ★
OKLAHOMA — Oklahoma City ★
TEXAS — Austin ★
MINNESOTA — Minneapolis ●, St. Paul ●
IOWA — Des Moines ★
MISSOURI — Jefferson City ★, St. Louis ●
ARKANSAS — Little Rock ★
LOUISIANA — Baton Rouge ★, New Orleans ●
MISSISSIPPI — Jackson ★
ALABAMA — Montgomery ★
WISCONSIN — Madison ★, Milwaukee ●
ILLINOIS — Springfield ★, Chicago ●
MICHIGAN — Lansing ★, Detroit ●
INDIANA — Indianapolis ●
OHIO — Columbus ★
KENTUCKY — Frankfort ★, Louisville ●
TENNESSEE — Nashville ★
GEORGIA — Atlanta ★
FLORIDA — Tallahassee ★
SOUTH CAROLINA — Columbia ★
NORTH CAROLINA — Raleigh ★
VIRGINIA — Richmond ★
W. VA — Charleston ★
PENN. — Harrisburg ★, Pittsburgh ●, Philadelphia ●
NEW YORK — Albany ★, Buffalo ●, New York ●
NEW JERSEY — Trenton ★, Jersey City ●, Newark ●
DELAWARE — Dover ★
MARYLAND — Annapolis ★, Baltimore ●, Washington, D.C. ✪
CONN. — Hartford ★
RI — Providence ★
MASS. — Boston ★
VT — Montpelier ★
NH — Concord ★
MAINE — Augusta ★

Rio Grande, Colorado R., Snake R., Columbia R., Missouri R., Arkansas R., Red R., Brazos R., Mississippi R., Ohio R., Tennessee R.

Great Salt Lake, Lake Superior, Lake Michigan, Lake Huron, Lake Erie, Lake Ontario, Lake Okeechobee

Scale: 0 200 400 km / 0 200 400 mi

Note that the areas with significant concentrations of foreign-born people tended to be in the newly opened regions of the West, in industrial cities of the north, and along both the Mexican and Canadian borders. Why were immigrants not generally attracted to the Southern states during this period?

34

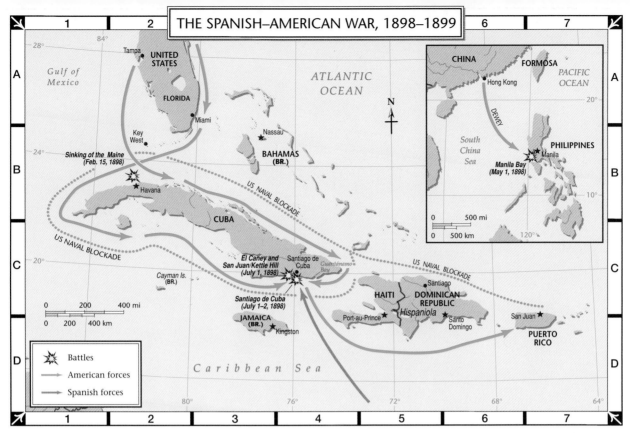

THE SPANISH–AMERICAN WAR, 1898–1899

Gulf of Mexico
Tampa
UNITED STATES
FLORIDA
Miami
Key West
ATLANTIC OCEAN
N

Sinking of the Maine (Feb. 15, 1898)
Havana
Nassau
BAHAMAS (BR.)
US NAVAL BLOCKADE
CUBA

El Caney and San Juan/Kettle Hill (July 1, 1898)
Santiago de Cuba
Guantánamo Bay
US NAVAL BLOCKADE

Cayman Is. (BR.)
Santiago de Cuba (July 1–2, 1898)
HAITI
DOMINICAN REPUBLIC
Santiago
Hispaniola

JAMAICA (BR.)
Kingston
Port-au-Prince
Santo Domingo
San Juan
PUERTO RICO

US NAVAL BLOCKADE

Caribbean Sea

Legend:
- Battles
- American forces
- Spanish forces

Inset map:
CHINA
FORMOSA
PACIFIC OCEAN
Hong Kong
DEWEY
South China Sea
PHILIPPINES
Manila
Manila Bay (May 1, 1898)
0 500 mi
0 500 km

The sinking of the battleship *Maine* prompted the United States to declare war on Spain in 1898. Meanwhile, the two nations dueled over another Spanish possession, the Philippines. The treaty ending the war granted Cuba its independence (although it remained an American protectorate until 1934), and assigned Puerto Rico, Guam, and the Philippines to American control. What was the political status of Haiti, the Dominican Republic, Jamaica and the Bahamas in 1899?

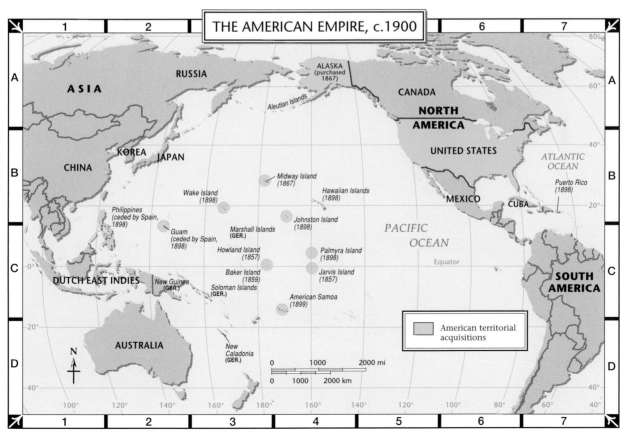

THE AMERICAN EMPIRE, c.1900

RUSSIA
ASIA
ALASKA (purchased 1867)
CANADA
Aleutian Islands
NORTH AMERICA
UNITED STATES

KOREA
JAPAN
CHINA
Midway Island (1867)
Hawaiian Islands (1898)
ATLANTIC OCEAN
Puerto Rico (1898)

Wake Island (1898)
MEXICO
CUBA

Philippines (ceded by Spain, 1898)
Johnston Island (1898)
PACIFIC OCEAN

Guam (ceded by Spain, 1898)
Marshall Islands (GER.)
Palmyra Island (1898)

Howland Island (1857)
Equator
SOUTH AMERICA

DUTCH EAST INDIES
New Guinea (GER.)
Baker Island (1859)
Soloman Islands (GER.)
Jarvis Island (1857)

American Samoa (1899)

AUSTRALIA
New Caladonia (GER.)
N
0 1000 2000 mi
0 1000 2000 km

American territorial acquisitions

Through warfare, annexation, and purchase, the United States had established itself as a Pacific power by the turn of the century. In addition to acquiring the future states of Alaska and Hawaii, the United States gained control over the Philippines, Puerto Rico, and numerous Pacific islands. Why were American imperial holdings concentrated in the Pacific Ocean rather than the Atlantic?

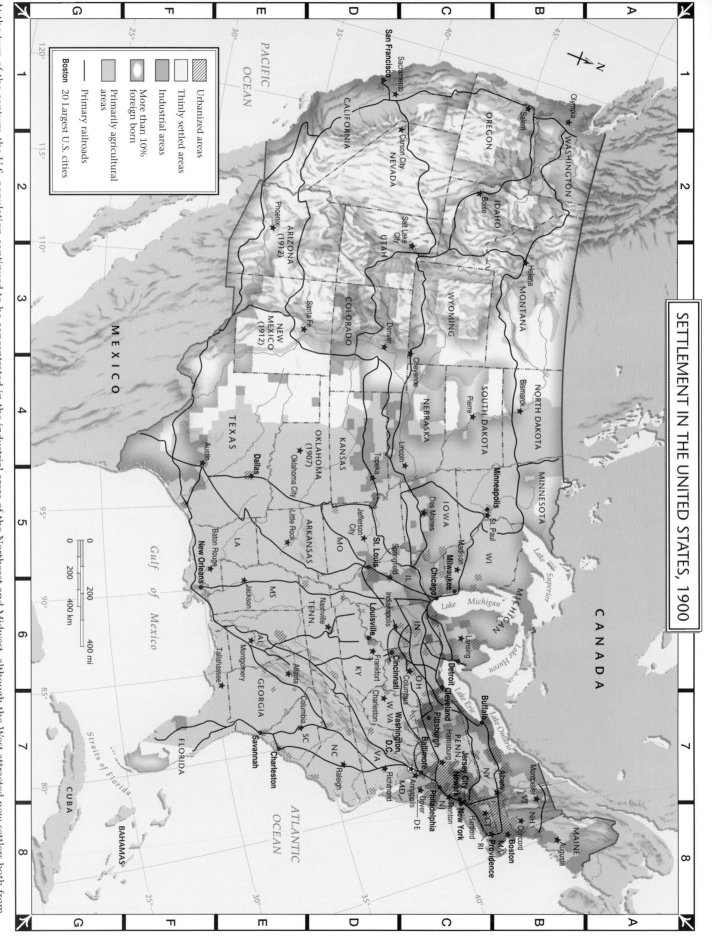

SETTLEMENT IN THE UNITED STATES, 1900

At the turn of the century, the U.S. population continued to be concentrated in the industrial areas of the Northeast and Midwest, although the West attracted new settlers both from America and abroad. The center of the nation's population in 1900 was in southeastern Indiana. In 1910 it would move across the states in which direction?

Legend:
- Urbanized areas
- Thinly settled areas
- Industrial areas
- More than 10% foreign born
- Primarily agricultural areas
- Primary railroads
- **Boston** 20 Largest U.S. cities

Scale: 0 200 400 km / 0 200 400 mi

MILESTONES IN EDUCATION

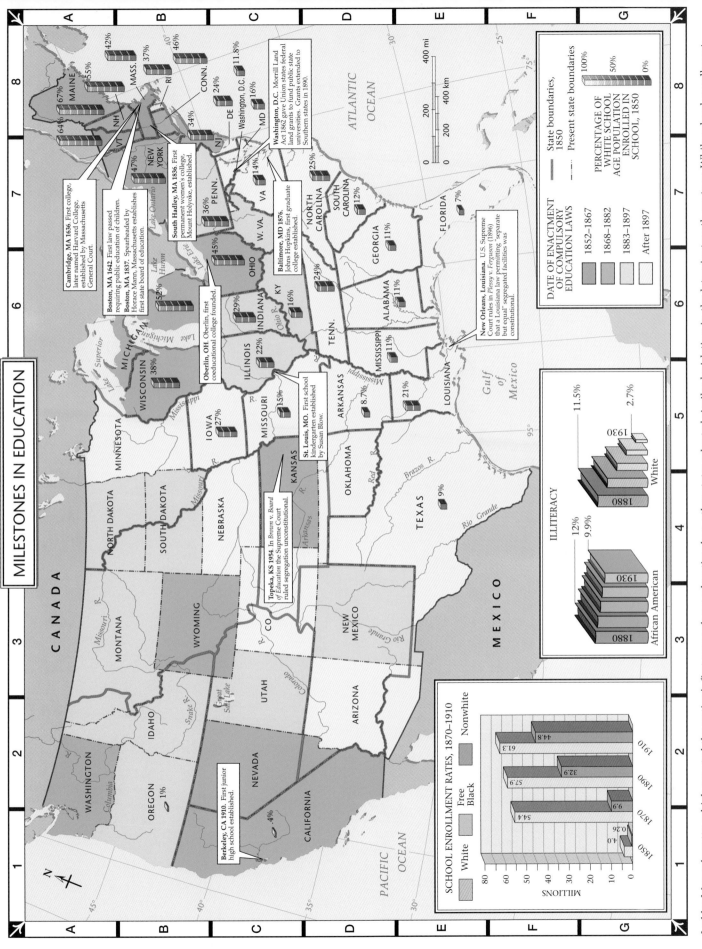

Cambridge, MA 1636. First college, later named Harvard College, established by Massachusetts General Court.

Boston, MA 1642. First law passed requiring public education of children.

Boston, MA 1837. Spearheaded by Horace Mann, Massachusetts establishes first state board of education.

South Hadley, MA 1836. First permanent women's college, Mount Holyoke, established.

Oberlin, OH. Oberlin, first coeducational college founded.

Baltimore, MD 1876. Johns Hopkins, first graduate college established.

Washington, D.C. Morrill Land Act 1862 gave Union states federal land grants to fund public state universities. Grants extended to Southern states in 1890.

New Orleans, Louisiana. U.S. Supreme Court rules in *Plessy v. Ferguson* (1896) that a Louisiana law permitting "separate but equal" segregated facilities was constitutional.

St. Louis, MO. First school kindergarten established by Susan Blow.

Topeka, KS 1954. In *Brown v. Board of Education* the Supreme Court ruled segregation unconstitutional.

Berkeley, CA 1910. First junior high school established.

PERCENTAGE OF WHITE SCHOOL AGE POPULATION ENROLLED IN SCHOOL, 1850

- 100%
- 50%
- 0%

State boundaries, 1850
Present state boundaries

DATE OF ENACTMENT OF COMPULSORY EDUCATION LAWS

- 1852–1867
- 1868–1882
- 1883–1897
- After 1897

State percentages
- MAINE 67%
- 55% / 42% (MASS.)
- 37% / 40% (MASS.)
- NH 64%
- VT
- RI 46%
- CONN. 24%
- DE 11.8% (Washington, D.C.)
- MD 16%
- NEW YORK 47%
- N.J. 34%
- PENN. 36%
- W. VA. 14%
- VA 25% (N.C.)
- OHIO 45%
- INDIANA 29%
- ILLINOIS 22%
- MICHIGAN 52%
- WISCONSIN 38%
- IOWA 27%
- MISSOURI 15%
- KY 16%
- TENN. 24%
- N.C. 25%
- S.C. 12%
- GEORGIA 11%
- ALABAMA 11%
- MISSISSIPPI 11%
- ARKANSAS 8.7%
- LOUISIANA 21%
- FLORIDA 7%
- TEXAS 9%
- OREGON 1%
- CALIFORNIA .4%

ILLITERACY

White: 1880 11.5%, 1930 2.7%
African American: 1880, 1930 — 12% / 9.9%

SCHOOL ENROLLMENT RATES, 1870–1910

(MILLIONS)

White | Free Black | Nonwhite

- 1850: 4.0 / 0.26
- 1870: 54.4 / 6.9
- 1890: 57.9 / 32.9
- 1910: 61.3 / 44.8

Map labels
CANADA, MEXICO, PACIFIC OCEAN, ATLANTIC OCEAN, Gulf of Mexico, Lake Superior, Lake Michigan, Lake Huron, Lake Erie, Lake Ontario, Mississippi R., Missouri R., Ohio R., Arkansas R., Red R., Brazos R., Rio Grande, Columbia R., Snake R., Great Salt Lake

States: WASHINGTON, OREGON, IDAHO, MONTANA, NORTH DAKOTA, SOUTH DAKOTA, MINNESOTA, WYOMING, NEVADA, UTAH, COLORADO, NEBRASKA, KANSAS, OKLAHOMA, NEW MEXICO, ARIZONA, TEXAS

400 mi / 400 km
0 200 / 0 200

Led by Massachusetts, which enacted the nation's first compulsory education law, other states adopted similar legislation in the late nineteenth century. While school enrollment increased and illiteracy declined, these gains were not shared equally, as African Americans continued to be excluded from white schools until the 1950s. What geographic factors would encourage the diffusion of ideas like compulsory education?

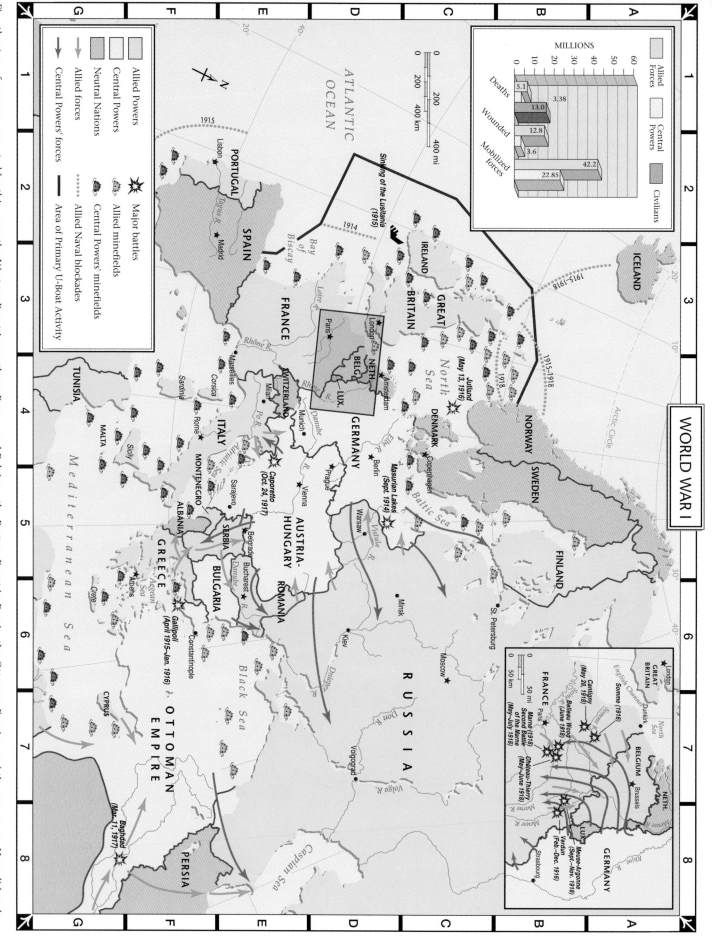

Five theaters of war are suggested by this map: the Western Front in northern France and Belgium, the Eastern Front in Russia, the Ottoman Empire, and the war at sea. How did each of these struggles affect the United States?

WORLD WAR I

Legend

Major battles ✸

Allied forces 🪖

Central Powers' forces 🪖

Allied Naval blockades ⋯⋯⋯

Area of Primary U-Boat Activity ━━━

Allied Powers →

Central Powers →

Allied forces →

Central Powers' forces →

Neutral Nations

Allied minefields

Central Powers' minefields

Casualties (inset chart)

MILLIONS — Allied Forces / Central Powers / Civilians

Deaths: 5.1, 3.38, 13.0

Wounded: 12.8, 3.6

Mobilized forces: 42.2, 22.85

Map labels

ATLANTIC OCEAN

Sinking of the Lusitania (1915)

PORTUGAL — Lisbon, Madrid
SPAIN
FRANCE — Paris
GREAT BRITAIN — London
IRELAND
NETH., BELG., LUX.
GERMANY — Berlin, Munich, Prague
DENMARK — Copenhagen
NORWAY, SWEDEN, FINLAND
ICELAND
North Sea
Baltic Sea
Arctic Circle

Jutland (May 13, 1916)
Masurian Lakes (Sept. 1914)
Warsaw
Vistula R.
Elbe R.
Danube R.
Rhône R., Rhine R., Loire R.

SWITZERLAND
ITALY — Milan, Rome
Corsica, Sardinia, Sicily
Caporetto (Oct. 24, 1917)
Adriatic Sea
Po R.
AUSTRIA-HUNGARY
MONTENEGRO, ALBANIA, SERBIA — Sarajevo, Belgrade
BULGARIA, ROMANIA — Bucharest
GREECE — Athens
Aegean Sea
Crete
Mediterranean Sea
TUNISIA, MALTA
CYPRUS
Black Sea
Gallipoli (April 1915–Jan. 1916)
Constantinople
OTTOMAN EMPIRE
Baghdad (Mar. 11, 1917)
PERSIA
Caspian Sea
Volga R., Don R., Dnieper R.

RUSSIA — Moscow, St. Petersburg, Minsk, Kiev, Volgograd

Inset map (Western Front, France)

FRANCE — Paris
GREAT BRITAIN — London, Dunkirk
BELGIUM — Brussels
NETH.
GERMANY — Strasbourg
LUX.
North Sea
English Channel
Somme R., Marne R., Meuse R., Rhine R.

Somme (1916)
Cantigny (May 28, 1918)
Belleau Wood (June 1918)
Marne (1918) / Second Battle of the Marne (May–July 1918)
Château-Thierry (May–June 1918)
Verdun (Feb.–Dec. 1916)
Meuse-Argonne (Sept.–Nov. 1918)

0   50 km
0   50 mi

N

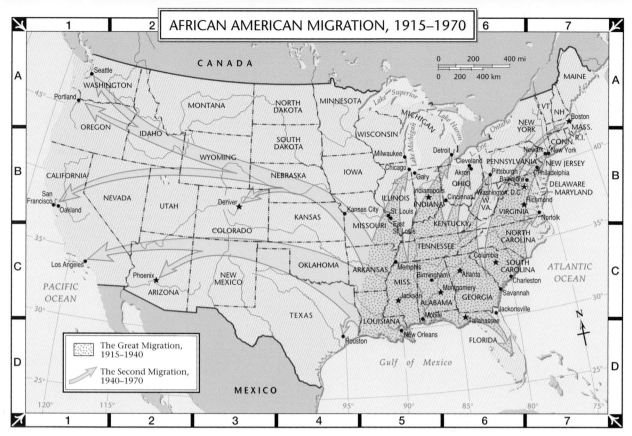

AFRICAN AMERICAN MIGRATION, 1915–1970

The Great Migration,
1915–1940

The Second Migration,
1940–1970

Facing pervasive racism and continuing economic hardship, many African Americans left the South in the early twenti-eth century. This Great Migration to the industrial cities of the North met the need for workers during World War I. A similar surge in migration, this time to the North and West, occurred during and after World War II. In the North, African Americans worked in low-paying jobs and were subjected to discrimination. From the indications on this map, which states were likely to have the lowest percentage of African-American citizens after 1970?

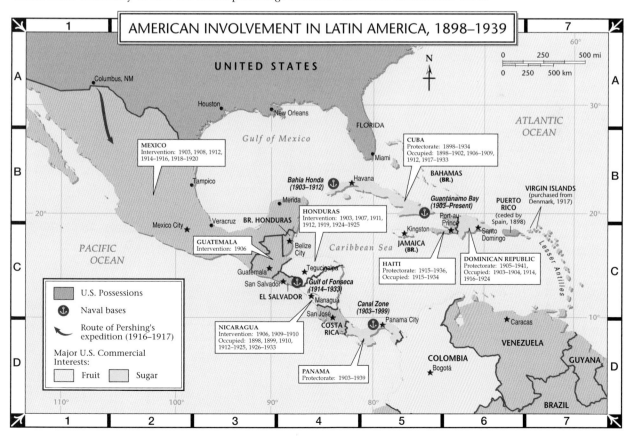

AMERICAN INVOLVEMENT IN LATIN AMERICA, 1898–1939

MEXICO
Intervention: 1903, 1908, 1912, 1914–1916, 1918–1920

CUBA
Protectorate: 1898–1934
Occupied: 1898–1902, 1906–1909, 1912, 1917–1933

VIRGIN ISLANDS
(purchased from Denmark, 1917)

PUERTO RICO
(ceded by Spain, 1898)

HONDURAS
Intervention: 1903, 1907, 1911, 1912, 1919, 1924–1925

GUATEMALA
Intervention: 1906

HAITI
Protectorate: 1915–1936,
Occupied: 1915–1934

DOMINICAN REPUBLIC
Protectorate: 1905–1941,
Occupied: 1903–1904, 1914, 1916–1924

NICARAGUA
Intervention: 1906, 1909–1910
Occupied: 1898, 1899, 1910, 1912–1925, 1926–1933

PANAMA
Protectorate: 1903–1939

Bahia Honda (1903–1912)

Guantánamo Bay (1903–Present)

Gulf of Fonseca (1914–1933)

Canal Zone (1903–1999)

U.S. Possessions

Naval bases

Route of Pershing's expedition (1916–1917)

Major U.S. Commercial Interests:

Fruit   Sugar

Having established a far-flung colonial empire, the United States attempted to exert dominance over its southern neighbors. A series of interventions and occupations followed as America sought to protect its political and economic interests in the Caribbean region. Which nations had the largest number of instances of American involvement in domestic politics?

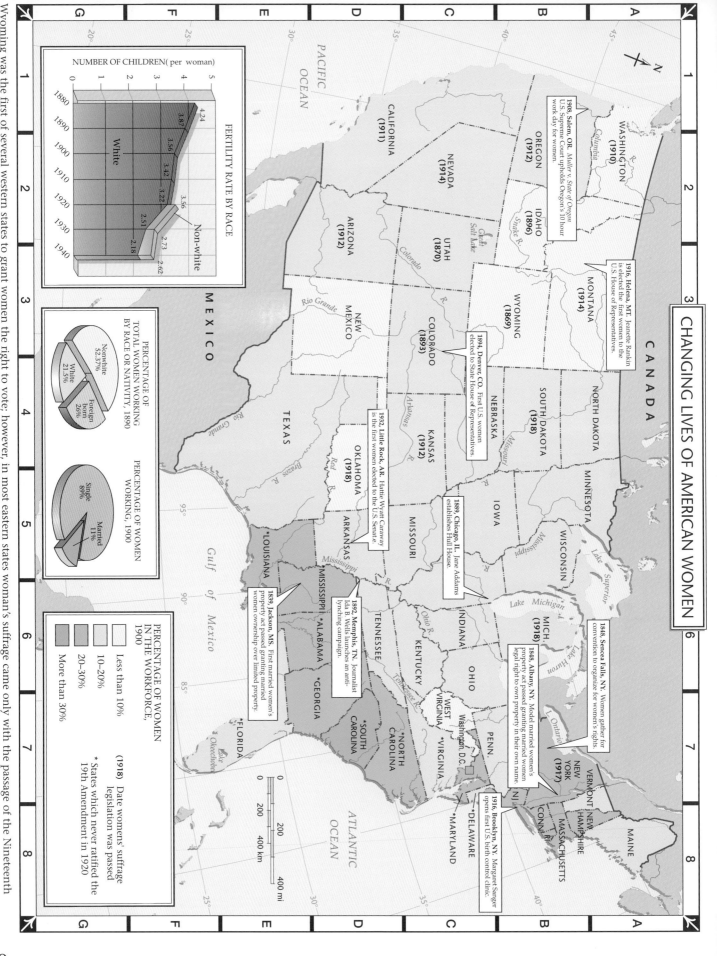

CHANGING LIVES OF AMERICAN WOMEN

Wyoming was the first of several western states to grant women the right to vote; however, in most eastern states woman's suffrage came only with the passage of the Nineteenth Amendment in 1920. The number of women in the workforce grew steadily to 18 percent by 1900, a figure which reflects an emphasis on industrial workers and ignores those more informally employed in agricultural and domestic occupations. How might one explain the higher percentage of women in the workforce in South Carolina and the Southern states in 1900? Would the same explanation hold true for New York and New England?

40

FERTILITY RATE BY RACE

NUMBER OF CHILDREN(per woman)

White
4.24
3.87
3.56
3.42
3.22
3.56
2.51
2.73
2.18
2.62

Non-white

1880
1890
1900
1910
1920
1930
1940

PERCENTAGE OF TOTAL WOMEN WORKING BY RACE OR NATIVITY, 1890

Nonwhite 52.37%
White 21.5%
Foreign born 26%

PERCENTAGE OF WOMEN WORKING, 1900

Single 89%
Married 11%

PERCENTAGE OF WOMEN IN THE WORKFORCE, 1900

Less than 10%
10-20%
20-30%
More than 30%

(1918) Date women's suffrage legislation was passed

* States which never ratified the 19th Amendment in 1920

0 200 400 km
0 200 400 mi

Map labels

WASHINGTON (1910)
OREGON (1912)
CALIFORNIA (1911)
NEVADA (1914)
IDAHO (1896)
MONTANA (1914)
UTAH (1870)
ARIZONA (1912)
WYOMING (1869)
COLORADO (1893)
NEW MEXICO
NORTH DAKOTA
SOUTH DAKOTA (1918)
NEBRASKA
KANSAS (1912)
OKLAHOMA (1918)
TEXAS
ARKANSAS
MISSOURI
IOWA
MINNESOTA
WISCONSIN
MICH. (1918)
*LOUISIANA
*MISSISSIPPI
*ALABAMA
*GEORGIA
TENNESSEE
KENTUCKY
INDIANA
OHIO
WEST VIRGINIA
*SOUTH CAROLINA
*NORTH CAROLINA
*VIRGINIA
*MARYLAND
*DELAWARE
PENN.
NEW YORK (1917)
*FLORIDA
Washington, D.C.
VERMONT
NEW HAMPSHIRE
MASSACHUSETTS
CONN.
N.J.
MAINE

CANADA
MEXICO
PACIFIC OCEAN
ATLANTIC OCEAN
Gulf of Mexico
Great Salt Lake
Lake Superior
Lake Michigan
Lake Huron
L. Ontario
Lake Okeechobee
Columbia R.
Snake R.
Colorado R.
Rio Grande
Rio Grande
Brazos R.
Red R.
Arkansas R.
Missouri R.
Mississippi R.
Ohio R.
Tennessee R.

Annotation boxes

1908, Salem, OR. Muller v. State of Oregon U.S. Supreme Court upholds Oregon's 10 hour work day for women.

1916, Helena, MT. Jeanette Rankin is elected the first women to the U.S. House of Representatives.

1894, Denver, CO. First U.S. women elected to State House of Representatives.

1932, Little Rock, AR. Hattie Wyatt Caraway is the first women elected to the U.S. Senate.

1889, Chicago, IL. Jane Addams establishes Hull House.

1892, Memphis, TN. Journalist Ida B. Wells launches an anti-lynching campaign.

1839, Jackson, MS. First married women's property act passed granting married women ownership over limited property.

1848, Seneca Falls, NY. Women gather for convention to organize for women's rights.

1848, Albany, NY. Model married women's property act passed granting married women legal right to own property in their own name.

1916, Brooklyn, NY. Margaret Sanger opens first U.S. birth control clinic.

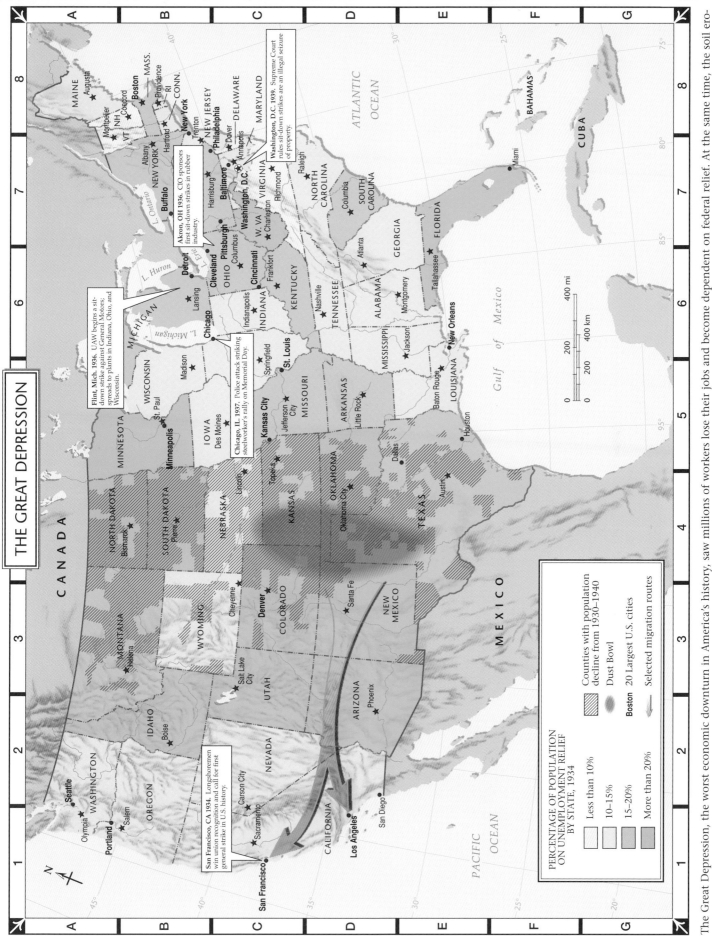

THE GREAT DEPRESSION

Flint, Mich. 1936. UAW begins a sit-down strike against General Motors; spreads to plants in Indiana, Ohio, and Wisconsin.

Akron, OH 1936. CIO sponsors first sit-down strikes in rubber industry.

Washington, D.C. 1939. Supreme Court rules sit-down strikes are an illegal seizure of property.

Chicago, IL. 1937. Police attack striking steelworker's rally on Memorial Day.

San Francisco, CA 1934. Longshoremen win union recognition and call for first general strike in U.S. history.

PERCENTAGE OF POPULATION ON UNEMPLOYMENT RELIEF BY STATE, 1934

- Less than 10%
- 10–15%
- 15–20%
- More than 20%

- Counties with population decline from 1930–1940
- Dust Bowl
- **Boston** 20 Largest U.S. cities
- Selected migration routes

400 mi
200   400 km

ATLANTIC OCEAN

PACIFIC OCEAN

Gulf of Mexico

CANADA

MEXICO

The Great Depression, the worst economic downturn in America's history, saw millions of workers lose their jobs and become dependent on federal relief. At the same time, the soil erosion, crop failures, and droughts of the Dust Bowl drove desperate farmers from the Plains states to look for work elsewhere, especially on the West Coast. Why is the 100th meridian often cited as a critical line in the 1930s?

41

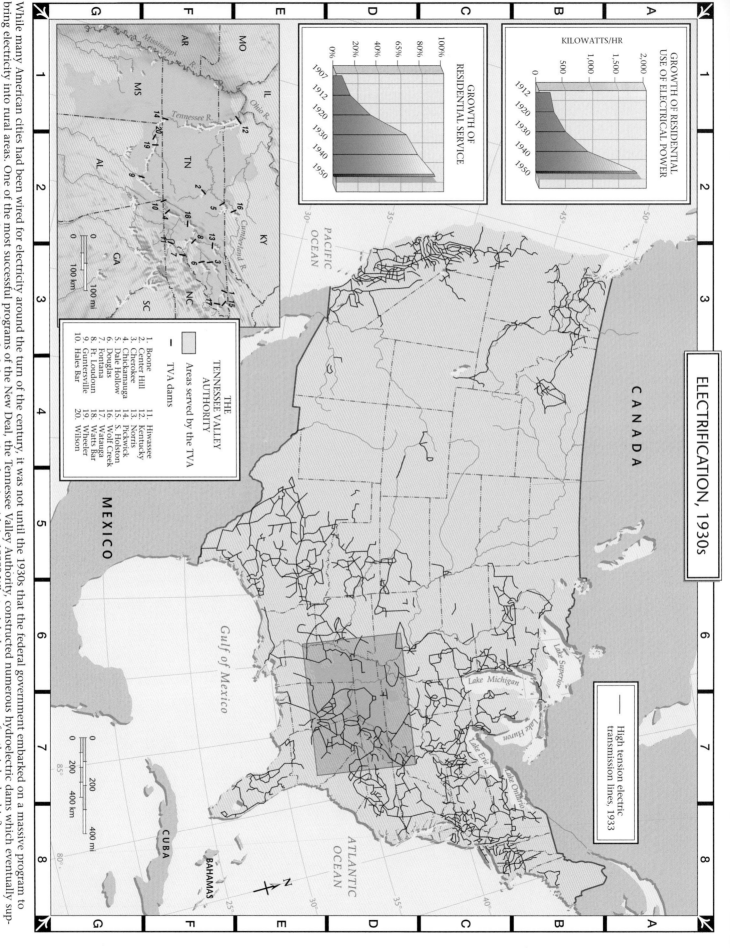

ELECTRIFICATION, 1930s

While many American cities had been wired for electricity around the turn of the century, it was not until the 1930s that the federal government embarked on a massive program to bring electricity into rural areas. One of the most successful programs of the New Deal, the Tennessee Valley Authority, constructed numerous hydroelectric dams which eventually supplied power for many communities. Which five states seem to have had the most extensive electric grids in 1833? What might be some reasons for their leadership?

GROWTH OF RESIDENTIAL USE OF ELECTRICAL POWER

KILOWATTS/HR

GROWTH OF RESIDENTIAL SERVICE

THE TENNESSEE VALLEY AUTHORITY

- Areas served by the TVA
- — TVA dams

1. Boone
2. Center Hill
3. Cherokee
4. Chickamauga
5. Dale Hollow
6. Douglas
7. Fontana
8. Ft. Loudoun
9. Guntersville
10. Hales Bar
11. Hiwassee
12. Kentucky
13. Norris
14. Pickwick
15. S. Holston
16. Wolf Creek
17. Watauga
18. Watts Bar
19. Wheeler
20. Wilson

— High tension electric transmission lines, 1933

42

WORLD WAR II ON THE HOME FRONT: WAR INDUSTRY AND RELOCATION

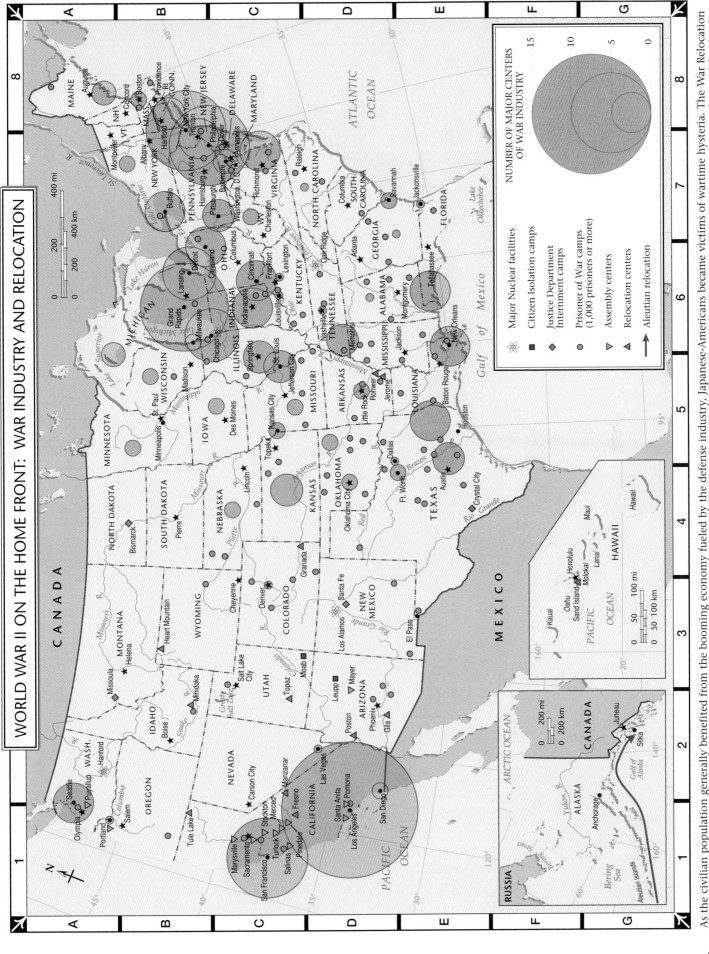

As the civilian population generally benefited from the booming economy fueled by the defense industry, Japanese-Americans became victims of wartime hysteria. The War Relocation Authority (WRA) removed thousands of Japanese Americans to temporary assembly centers before transporting them to remote relocation camps, where they were detained for the duration of the war. Why were war industries, POW camps, and relocation centers dispersed across the nation? What city had the greatest concentration of war industries?

43

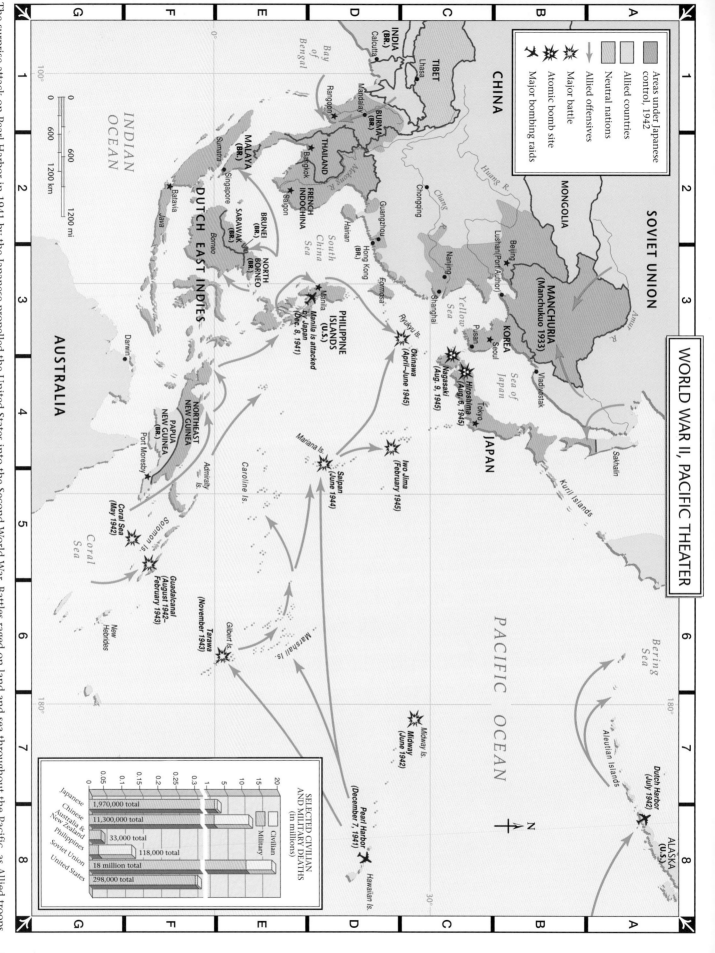

WORLD WAR II, PACIFIC THEATER

The surprise attack on Pearl Harbor in 1941 by the Japanese propelled the United States into the Second World War. Battles raged on land and sea throughout the Pacific, as Allied troops slowly reclaimed the Pacific Islands, Manchukuo, and Southeast Asia from Japanese occupation.

Legend:

- Areas under Japanese control, 1942
- Neutral nations
- Allied countries
- Allied nations
- Allied offensives
- Major bombing raids
- Atomic bomb site
- Major battle

Scale:
0   600   1200 km
0   600   1200 mi

SOVIET UNION

MONGOLIA

CHINA
- Beijing
- Lushan (Port Author)
- Nanjing
- Shanghai
- Chongqing
- Guangzhou
- Hong Kong (BR.)
- Hainan
- Vladivostak

MANCHURIA (Manchukuo 1933)

KOREA
- Pusan
- Seoul

JAPAN
- Tokyo
- Hiroshima (Aug. 6, 1945)
- Nagasaki (Aug. 9, 1945)

Sakhalin
Kuril Islands

Sea of Japan
Yellow Sea
Formosa

TIBET
- Lhasa

INDIA (BR.)
- Calcutta
- Mandalay
- Rangoon

BURMA (BR.)
Mekong R.

THAILAND
- Bangkok

FRENCH INDOCHINA
- Saigon

MALAYA (BR.)
- Sumatra
- Singapore

BRUNEI (BR.)
SARAWAK (BR.)
NORTH BORNEO (BR.)
Borneo

DUTCH EAST INDIES
- Batavia
- Java

Bay of Bengal
INDIAN OCEAN
South China Sea

PHILIPPINE ISLANDS (U.S.)
- Manila
- Manila is attacked by Japan (Dec. 8, 1941)

Ryukyu Is.
Okinawa (April–June 1945)

Iwo Jima (February 1945)

Mariana Is.
Saipan (June 1944)

Caroline Is.

Admiralty Is.

PAPUA NEW GUINEA (BR.)
NORTHEAST NEW GUINEA
- Port Moresby

Coral Sea (May 1942)
Coral Sea
Solomon Is.

Guadalcanal (August 1942–February 1943)

New Hebrides

Tarawa (November 1943)
Gilbert Is.
Marshall Is.

AUSTRALIA
- Darwin

PACIFIC OCEAN

Midway Is.
Midway (June 1942)

Pearl Harbor (December 7, 1941)
Hawaiian Is.

Bering Sea
Aleutian Islands

Dutch Harbor (July 1942)
ALASKA (U.S.)

Amur R.

N

SELECTED CIVILIAN AND MILITARY DEATHS (in millions)

	Military	Civilian
Japanese		1,970,000 total
Chinese		11,300,000 total
Australia & New Zealand		33,000 total
Philippines		118,000 total
Soviet Union		18 million total
United States		298,000 total

Scale values: 0, 0.05, 0.1, 0.15, 0.2, 0.25, 0.3 and 1, 5, 10, 15, 20

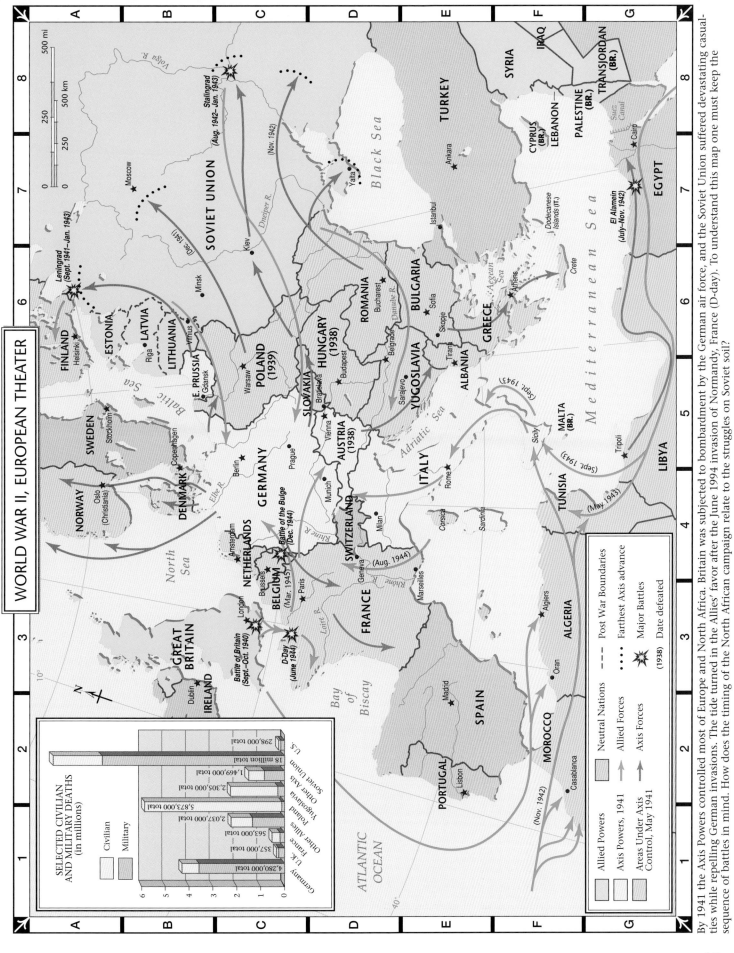

WORLD WAR II, EUROPEAN THEATER

SELECTED CIVILIAN AND MILITARY DEATHS (in millions)

Civilian
Military

Germany 4,280,000 total
U.K. 357,000 total
France 563,000 total
Other Allies 2,037,000 total
Poland 5,873,000 total
Yugoslavia 2,305,000 total
Other Axis 1,469,000 total
Soviet Union 18 million total
U.S. 298,000 total

Legend:
- Allied Powers
- Axis Powers, 1941
- Areas Under Axis Control, May 1941
- Neutral Nations
- Allied Forces
- Axis Forces
- — — — Post War Boundaries
- • • • • Farthest Axis advance
- Major Battles
- (1938) Date defeated

By 1941 the Axis Powers controlled most of Europe and North Africa. Britain was subjected to bombardment by the German air force, and the Soviet Union suffered devastating casualties while repelling German invasions. The tide turned in the Allies' favor after the June 1994 invasion of Normandy, France (D-day). To understand this map one must keep the sequence of battles in mind. How does the timing of the North African campaign relate to the struggles on Soviet soil?

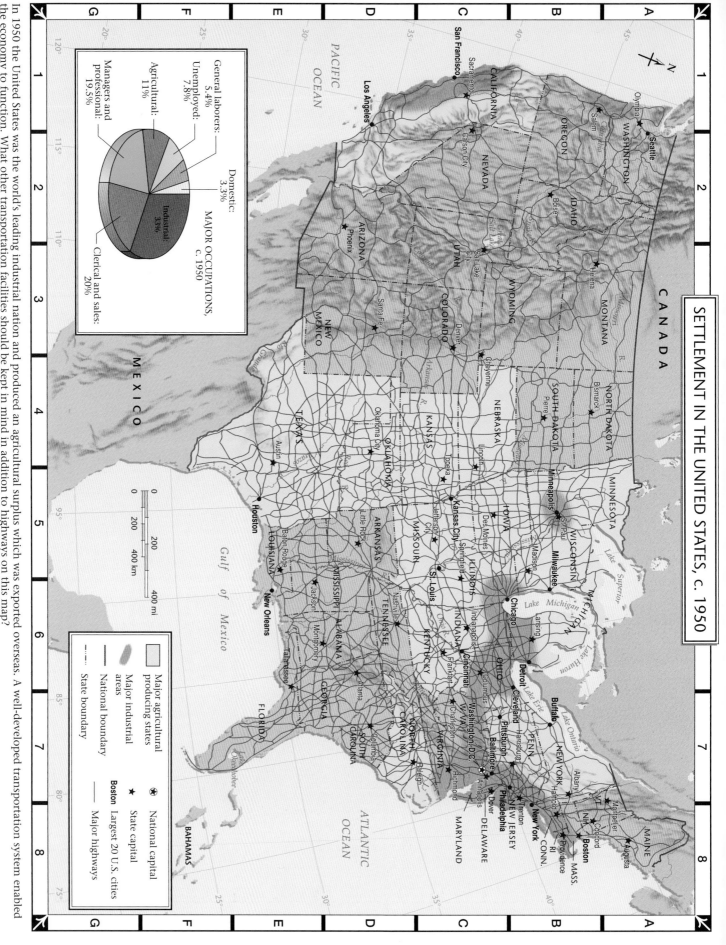

SETTLEMENT IN THE UNITED STATES, c. 1950

In 1950 the United States was the world's leading industrial nation and produced an agricultural surplus which was exported overseas. A well-developed transportation system enabled the economy to function. What other transportation facilities should be kept in mind in addition to highways on this map?

MAJOR OCCUPATIONS, c. 1950

- General laborers: 5.4%
- Unemployed: 7.8%
- Agricultural: 11%
- Managers and professional: 19.5%
- Clerical and sales: 20%
- Industrial: 33%
- Domestic: 3.3%

Legend

- ⊛ National capital
- ★ State capital
- **Boston** Largest 20 U.S. cities
- Major agricultural producing states
- Major industrial areas
- — — National boundary
- ⸺ State boundary
- ⸺ Major highways

Scale: 0 200 400 km / 0 200 400 mi

COLD WAR IN EUROPE, 1950

During the Cold War, the United States and its Western Allies formed the North Atlantic Treaty Organization (NATO) to confront the perceived threat from the Soviet Union and its allies (the Warsaw Pact). An "Iron Curtain" divided the continent of Europe into East and West. Germany, defeated during World War II, was partitioned between the two rival blocs. Berlin, the German capital, was also divided into four occupation zones. How might this have led to friction after 1950?

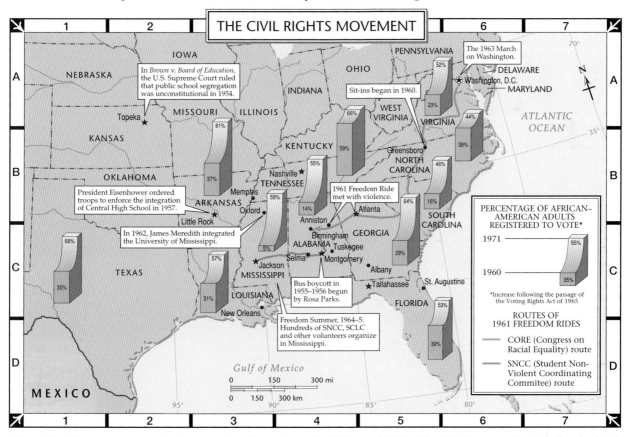

THE CIVIL RIGHTS MOVEMENT

The civil rights movement gained momentum throughout the 1950s and 1960s. The U.S. Supreme Court declared school segregation unconstitutional in Brown v. Board of Education; Rosa Parks refused to give up her seat on a Montgomery bus and sparked a bus boycott; the Freedom Rides drew attention to the problem of segregation; and the passage of the Voting Rights Act led to a dramatic increase in the number of African-American voters in the South. In which states did the increase in African-American voters between 1960 and 1971 probably have the greatest impact?

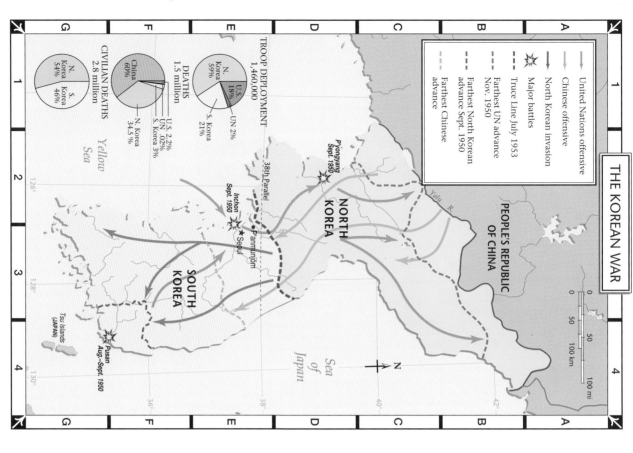

THE KOREAN WAR

When North Korea invaded South Korea in 1950, United Nations (UN) troops, commanded by General Douglas MacArthur, managed to drive them back to the Chinese border. This victory was short-lived, however, as Chinese troops entered the war, pushing the UN troops back to the south. Thousands of soldiers and millions of Korean civilians were killed in the conflict, which ended with the 1953 armistice that set the dividing line between the two countries in nearly the same place it had been before the war. How many times did Seoul change hands during the conflict?

United Nations offensive
Chinese offensive
North Korean invasion
Major battles
Farthest North Korean advance Nov. 1950
Farthest UN advance Sept. 1950
Truce Line July 1953
Farthest North Korean advance Sept. 1950
Farthest Chinese advance

TROOP DEPLOYMENT
1,460,000
N. Korea 59%
U.S. 18%
UN 2%
S. Korea 21%

DEATHS
1.5 million
China 60%
N. Korea 34.5%
U.S. 2.2%
UN .02%
S. Korea 3%

CIVILIAN DEATHS
2.8 million
N. Korea 54%
S. Korea 46%

PEOPLE'S REPUBLIC OF CHINA

NORTH KOREA

SOUTH KOREA

Pyongyang Sept. 1950
Inchon Sept. 1950
Seoul
Panmunjom
38th Parallel
Pusan Aug.–Sept. 1950
Tsu Islands (JAPAN)

Yellow Sea
Sea of Japan

Yalu R.

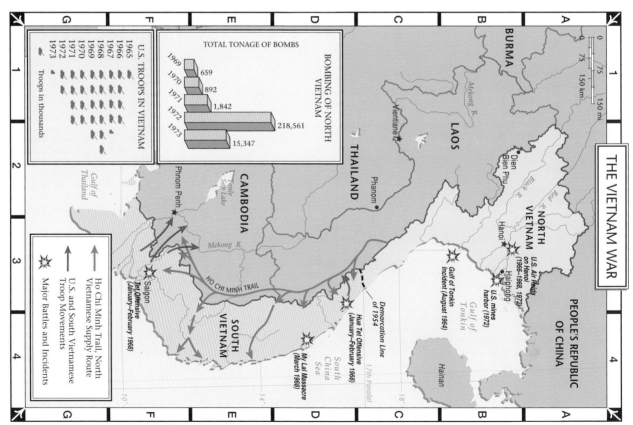

THE VIETNAM WAR

Although supplying financial assistance and military advisors to South Vietnam for years, the United States became directly involved in the Southeast Asia war following the Gulf of Tonkin incident in 1964. Despite the commitment of thousands of troops and massive bombing raids on North Vietnam, the Americans were unable to make much progress. The tide turned decisively after the North Vietnamese Tet offensive in 1968. Was China a factor in the Vietnam war? Compare the situation to that of the Korean War.

U.S. TROOPS IN VIETNAM
1965
1966
1967
1968
1969
1970
1971
1972
1973
Troops in thousands

TOTAL TONAGE OF BOMBS
BOMBING OF NORTH VIETNAM
1969 659
1970 892
1971 1,842
1972 218,561
1973 15,347

Ho Chi Minh Trail, North Vietnamese Supply Route
U.S. and South Vietnamese Troop Movements
Major Battles and Incidents

BURMA
LAOS
THAILAND
CAMBODIA
NORTH VIETNAM
SOUTH VIETNAM
PEOPLE'S REPUBLIC OF CHINA

Vientiane
Phanom
Phnom Penh
Saigon
Dien Bien Phu
Hanoi
Haiphong
Tonle Sap Lake
Mekong R.
Gulf of Thailand
Gulf of Tonkin
South China Sea
Hainan

U.S. Air Raids on Hanoi (1966–1968, 1972)
U.S. mines harbor (1972)
Gulf of Tonkin Incident (August 1964)
Demarcation Line of 1954
Hue Tet Offensive (January–February 1968)
Tet Offensive (January–February 1968)
My Lai Massacre (March 1968)
HO CHI MINH TRAIL
17th Parallel
Black R.
Red R.
Mekong R.

48

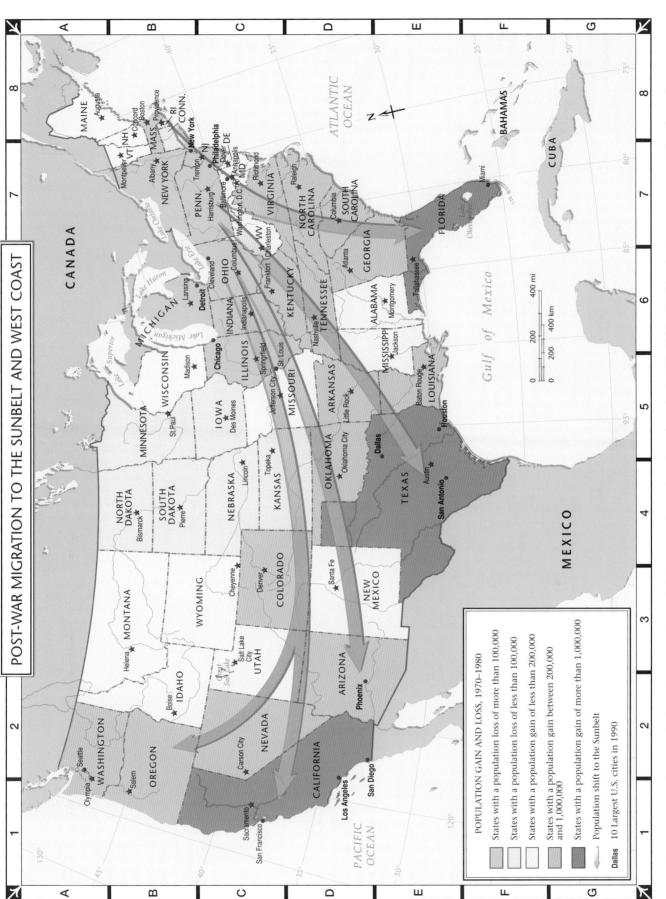

POST-WAR MIGRATION TO THE SUNBELT AND WEST COAST

POPULATION GAIN AND LOSS, 1970–1980

- States with a population loss of more than 100,000
- States with a population loss of less than 100,000
- States with a population gain of less than 200,000
- States with a population gain between 200,000 and 1,000,000
- States with a population gain of more than 1,000,000
- Population shift to the Sunbelt
- **Dallas** 10 Largest U.S. cities in 1990

Many Americans were drawn to the West Coast and the Sunbelt (states to the south and southwest) after World War II. This migration was prompted by diverse factors, including the employment opportunities offered by the growing defense-related industries in these regions, and the development of air conditioning, which made residence in these hotter climates more pleasant. The burgeoning populations of these states increased their political power at the expense of the declining Midwest and Northeast. Were the shifts in population during this period also characterized by a movement from interior regions to coastal areas?

49

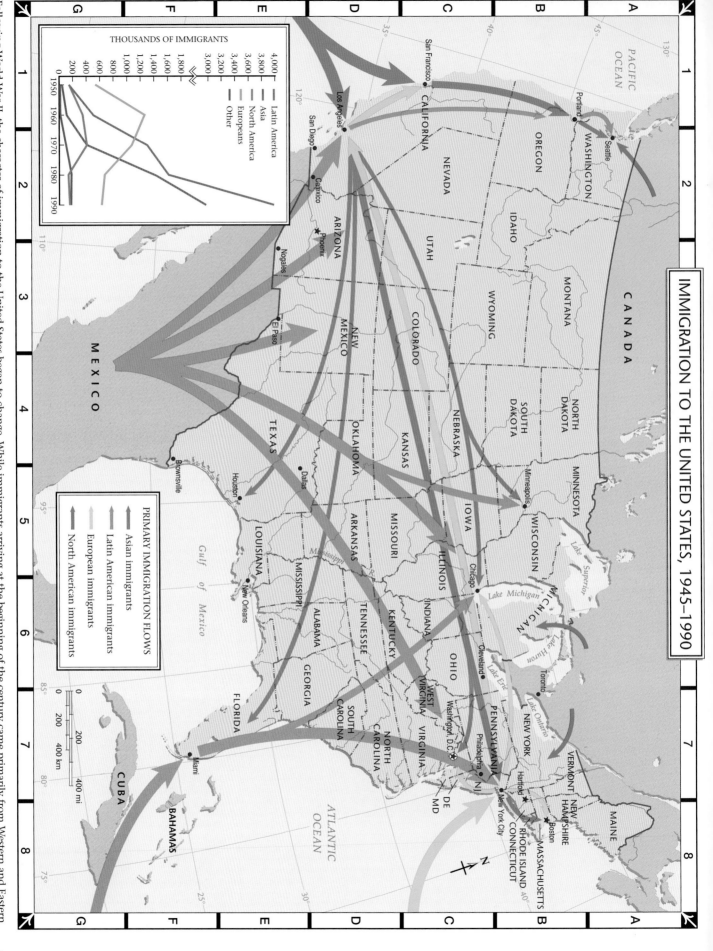

IMMIGRATION TO THE UNITED STATES, 1945–1990

THOUSANDS OF IMMIGRANTS

- Latin America
- Asia
- North America
- Europeans
- Other

PRIMARY IMMIGRATION FLOWS

- Asian immigrants
- Latin American immigrants
- European immigrants
- North American immigrants

Following World War II, the character of immigration to the United States began to change. While immigrants arriving at the beginning of the century came primarily from Western and Eastern Europe, the latter half of the century showed increasing numbers coming from Asia and Latin America. Which cities served as major gateways for immigrants during this period? Why?

50

SETTLEMENT IN THE UNITED STATES, c. 1998

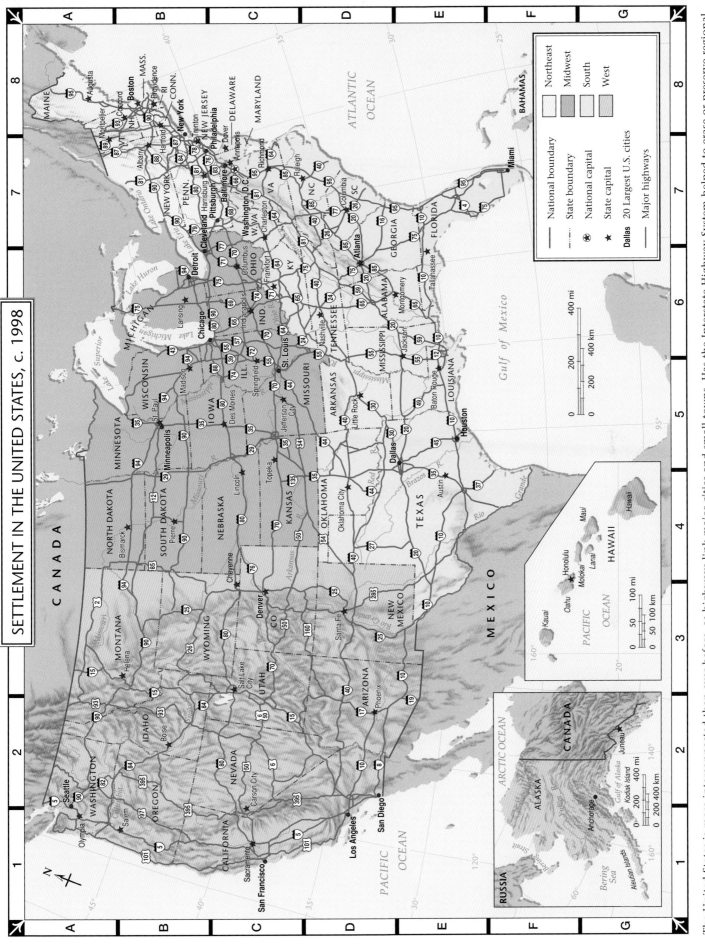

The United States is more interconnected than ever before, as highways link major cities and small towns. Has the Interstate Highway System helped to erase or preserve regional differences in the United States?

51

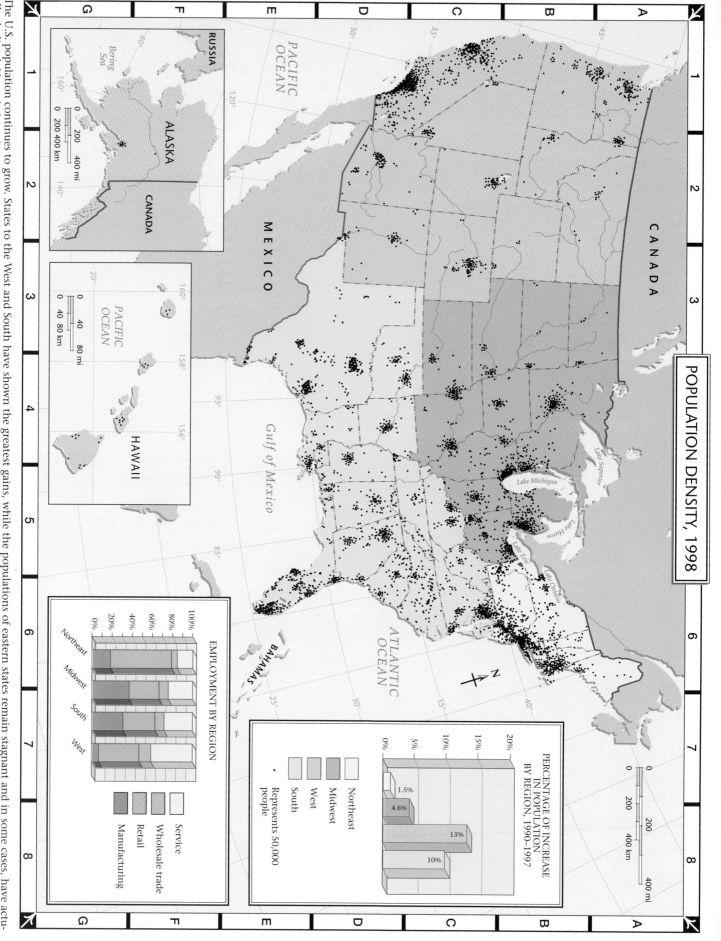

POPULATION DENSITY, 1998

RUSSIA

ALASKA

CANADA

Bering Sea

0 200 400 km
0 200 400 mi

PACIFIC OCEAN

HAWAII

0 40 80 km
0 40 80 mi

PACIFIC OCEAN

MEXICO

Gulf of Mexico

CANADA

Lake Superior
Lake Michigan
Lake Huron
Lake Erie
Lake Ontario

BAHAMAS

ATLANTIC OCEAN

0 200 400 km
0 200 400 mi

EMPLOYMENT BY REGION

100%
80%
60%
40%
20%
0%

Northeast
Midwest
South
West

Service
Wholesale trade
Retail
Manufacturing

PERCENTAGE OF INCREASE IN POPULATION BY REGION, 1990–1997

20%
15%
10%
5%
0%

South
West
Midwest
Northeast

• Represents 50,000 people

1.5%
4.6%
13%
10%

The U.S. population continues to grow. States to the West and South have shown the greatest gains, while the populations of eastern states remain stagnant and in some cases, have actually declined. Nevertheless, the people in the U.S. remain clustered in metropolitan areas. Note the "Bowash" megalopolis between the Boston and Washington areas.

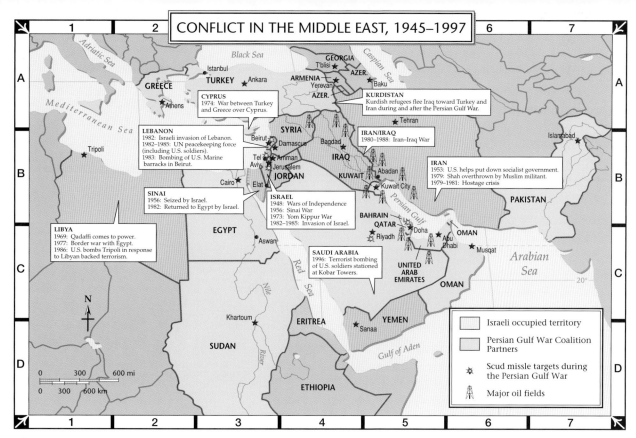

CONFLICT IN THE MIDDLE EAST, 1945–1997

CYPRUS
1974: War between Turkey and Greece over Cyprus.

KURDISTAN
Kurdish refugees flee Iraq toward Turkey and Iran during and after the Persian Gulf War.

LEBANON
1982: Israeli invasion of Lebanon.
1982–1985: UN peacekeeping force (including U.S. soldiers).
1983: Bombing of U.S. Marine barracks in Beirut.

IRAN/IRAQ
1980–1988: Iran–Iraq War

IRAN
1953: U.S. helps put down socialist government.
1979: Shah overthrown by Muslim militant.
1979–1981: Hostage crisis

SINAI
1956: Seized by Israel.
1982: Returned to Egypt by Israel.

ISRAEL
1948: Wars of Independence
1956: Sinai War
1973: Yom Kippur War
1982–1985: Invasion of Israel.

LIBYA
1969: Qadaffi comes to power.
1977: Border war with Egypt.
1986: U.S. bombs Tripoli in response to Libyan backed terrorism.

SAUDI ARABIA
1996: Terrorist bombing of U.S. soldiers stationed at Kobar Towers.

Legend:
- Israeli occupied territory
- Persian Gulf War Coalition Partners
- Scud missle targets during the Persian Gulf War
- Major oil fields

The United States has become involved in Middle Eastern conflicts by supporting its traditional ally Israel; by combating terrorist forces in Libya, Iran, and Lebanon; and most recently by repelling the Iraqi invasion of Kuwait. How did the American need to import oil affect U.S. policy in the Middle East during this period?

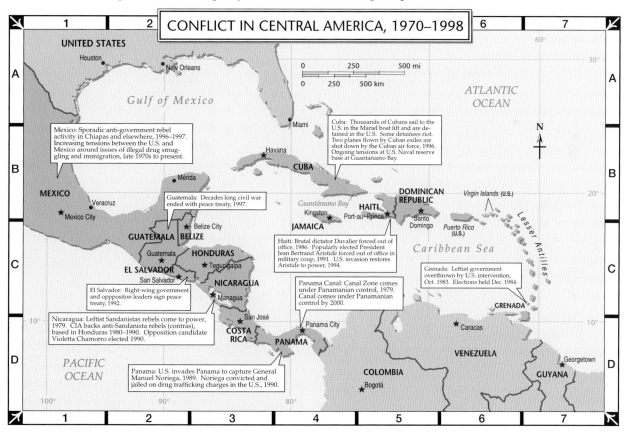

CONFLICT IN CENTRAL AMERICA, 1970–1998

Mexico: Sporadic anti-government rebel activity in Chiapas and elsewhere, 1996–1997. Increasing tensions between the U.S. and Mexico around issues of illegal drug smuggling and immigration, late 1970s to present.

Cuba: Thousands of Cubans sail to the U.S. in the Mariel boat lift and are detained in the U.S. Some detainees riot. Two planes flown by Cuban exiles are shot down by the Cuban air force, 1996. Ongoing tensions at U.S. Naval reserve base at Guantanamo Bay.

Guatemala: Decades long civil war ended with peace treaty, 1997.

Haiti: Brutal dictator Duvalier forced out of office, 1986. Popularly elected President Jean Bertrand Aristide forced out of office in military coup, 1991. U.S. invasion restores Aristide to power, 1994.

Grenada: Leftist government overthrown by U.S. intervention, Oct. 1983. Elections held Dec. 1984.

Panama Canal: Canal Zone comes under Panamanian control, 1979. Canal comes under Panamanian control by 2000.

El Salvador: Right-wing government and opppositon leaders sign peace treaty, 1992.

Nicaragua: Leftist Sandanistas rebels come to power, 1979. CIA backs anti-Sandanista rebels (contras), based in Honduras 1980–1990. Opposition candidate Violetta Chamorro elected 1990.

Panama: U.S. invades Panama to capture General Manuel Noriega, 1989. Noriega convicted and jailed on drug trafficking charges in the U.S., 1990.

Viewing the Western Hemisphere as its special zone of influence, the United States has often become involved in Central American conflicts. In addition to applying diplomatic pressure on issues of drugs and immigration, the U.S. government has often taken more active role in influencing its southern neighbors. Covert assistance to anti-communist rebels and direct military intervention have been used to ensure the establishment of regimes more friendly to the United States. How might the location of the places in the Caribbean have effected the geopolitical situation? Is the Panama Canal east or west of Miami? Which capital is closest to Granada: Mexico City, Brasilia or Washington?

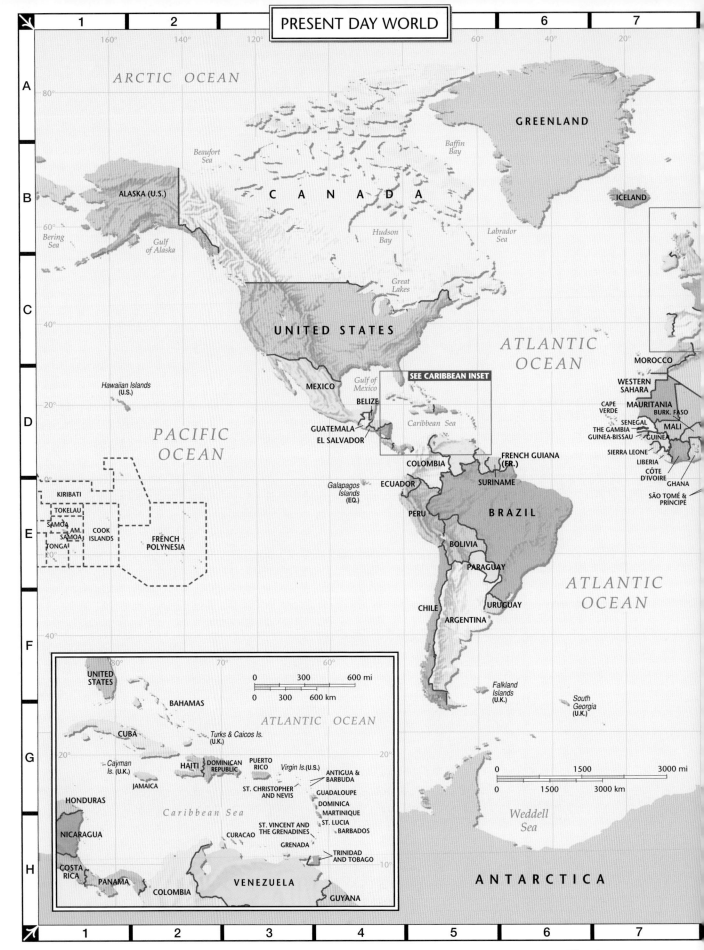

| | 1 | 2 | | | 6 | 7 |

ARCTIC OCEAN

GREENLAND

80°

Beaufort Sea

Baffin Bay

C A N A D A

ALASKA (U.S.)

ICELAND

60°

Bering Sea

Gulf of Alaska

Hudson Bay

Labrador Sea

Great Lakes

ATLANTIC OCEAN

40°

UNITED STATES

MOROCCO

Hawaiian Islands (U.S.)

SEE CARIBBEAN INSET

WESTERN SAHARA

20°

MEXICO

Gulf of Mexico

BELIZE

Caribbean Sea

CAPE VERDE

MAURITANIA

BURK. FASO

PACIFIC OCEAN

GUATEMALA

SENEGAL

MALI

THE GAMBIA

GUINEA-BISSAU

GUINEA

EL SALVADOR

SIERRA LEONE

LIBERIA

COLOMBIA

FRENCH GUIANA (FR.)

CÔTE D'IVOIRE

GHANA

0°

Galapagos Islands (EQ.)

ECUADOR

SURINAME

SÃO TOMÉ & PRÍNCIPE

KIRIBATI

TOKELAU

PERU

BRAZIL

SAMOA

AM. SAMOA

COOK ISLANDS

FRENCH POLYNESIA

TONGA

BOLIVIA

20°

PARAGUAY

ATLANTIC OCEAN

CHILE

URUGUAY

ARGENTINA

40°

Falkland Islands (U.K.)

South Georgia (U.K.)

| | | 1 | 2 | 3 | | 4 | 5 | | 6 | 7 |

UNITED STATES

80°

70°

60°

0   300   600 mi

0   300   600 km

BAHAMAS

ATLANTIC OCEAN

CUBA

Turks & Caicos Is. (U.K.)

20°

20°

Cayman Is. (U.K.)

HAITI

DOMINICAN REPUBLIC

PUERTO RICO

Virgin Is.(U.S.)

ANTIGUA & BARBUDA

JAMAICA

ST. CHRISTOPHER AND NEVIS

GUADALOUPE

0   1500   3000 mi

DOMINICA

HONDURAS

MARTINIQUE

0   1500   3000 km

Caribbean Sea

ST. VINCENT AND THE GRENADINES

ST. LUCIA

BARBADOS

Weddell Sea

NICARAGUA

CURACAO

GRENADA

COSTA RICA

TRINIDAD AND TOBAGO

PANAMA

VENEZUELA

A N T A R C T I C A

COLOMBIA

GUYANA

The areas on this political map of the world are greatly distorted by the Mercator projection. This image exaggerates the sizes of the countries as they get closer to the poles. How many nations have territory above 40

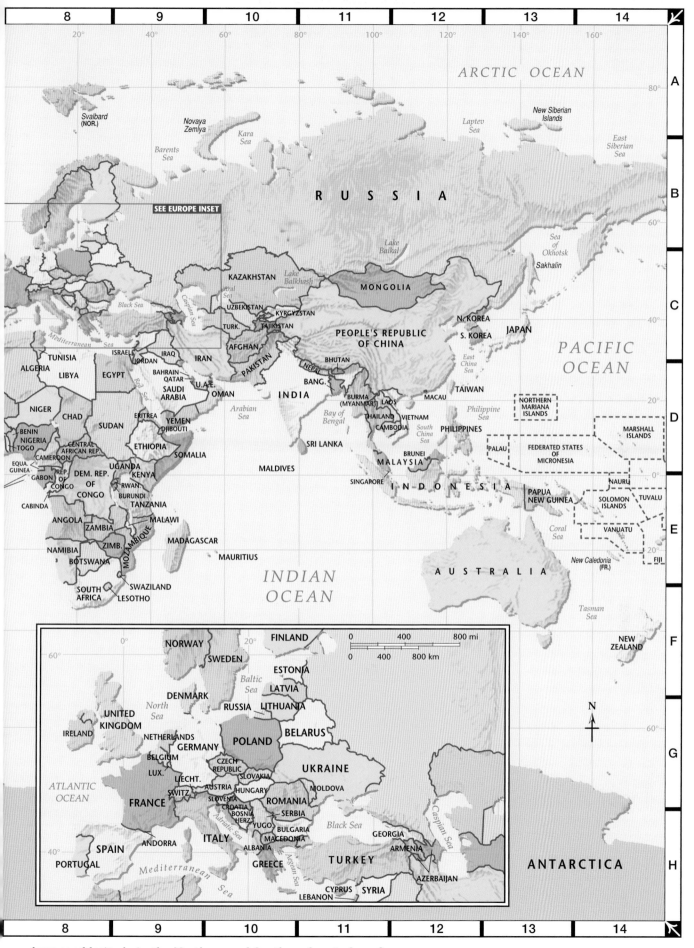

20° 40° 60° 80° 100° 120° 140° 160°

ARCTIC OCEAN

A

80°

Svalbard
(NOR.)

Novaya
Zemlya

Kara
Sea

Laptev
Sea

New Siberian
Islands

East
Siberian
Sea

Barents
Sea

B

60°

R U S S I A

SEE EUROPE INSET

Lake
Baikal

Sea
of
Okhotsk

Sakhalin

KAZAKHSTAN

Lake
Balkhash

MONGOLIA

Aral
Sea

Caspian Sea

Black Sea

C

40°

UZBEKISTAN

KYRGYZSTAN

N. KOREA

JAPAN

Mediterranean Sea

TURK.

TAJIKISTAN

S. KOREA

PACIFIC
OCEAN

TUNISIA

ISRAEL

IRAQ

IRAN

AFGHAN.

PEOPLE'S REPUBLIC
OF CHINA

East
China
Sea

ALGERIA

LIBYA

JORDAN

PAKISTAN

BHUTAN

Red Sea

EGYPT

BAHRAIN
QATAR

U.A.E.

NEPAL

BANG.

TAIWAN

MACAU

Philippine
Sea

D

20°

SAUDI
ARABIA

OMAN

INDIA

BURMA
(MYANMAR)

LAOS

NORTHERN
MARIANA
ISLANDS

NIGER

CHAD

SUDAN

Arabian
Sea

Bay of
Bengal

THAILAND

VIETNAM

CAMBODIA

South
China
Sea

PHILIPPINES

MARSHALL
ISLANDS

BENIN

ERITREA

YEMEN

SRI LANKA

NIGERIA

DJIBOUTI

0°

TOGO

CENTRAL
AFRICAN REP.

ETHIOPIA

SOMALIA

MALDIVES

BRUNEI

PALAU

FEDERATED STATES
OF
MICRONESIA

CAMEROON

EQUA.
GUINEA

UGANDA

KENYA

MALAYSIA

NAURU

GABON

REP.
OF
CONGO

DEM. REP.
OF
CONGO

RWAN.

BURUNDI

SINGAPORE

I N D O N E S I A

SOLOMON
ISLANDS

TUVALU

CABINDA

TANZANIA

PAPUA
NEW GUINEA

E

ANGOLA

MALAWI

Coral
Sea

VANUATU

20°

ZAMBIA

MADAGASCAR

MOZAMBIQUE

ZIMB.

MAURITIUS

A U S T R A L I A

New Caledonia
(FR.)

FIJI

NAMIBIA

BOTSWANA

INDIAN
OCEAN

SOUTH
AFRICA

SWAZILAND

LESOTHO

Tasman
Sea

F

NEW
ZEALAND

0° 20° FINLAND

NORWAY

SWEDEN

0 400 800 mi

0 400 800 km

60°

DENMARK

ESTONIA

Baltic
Sea

LATVIA

RUSSIA

LITHUANIA

N

North
Sea

UNITED
KINGDOM

G

IRELAND

NETHERLANDS

GERMANY

POLAND

BELARUS

60°

BELGIUM

LUX.

CZECH
REPUBLIC

SLOVAKIA

UKRAINE

ATLANTIC
OCEAN

LIECHT.

SWITZ.

AUSTRIA

HUNGARY

MOLDOVA

Caspian Sea

FRANCE

SLOVENIA

CROATIA

BOSNIA
HERZ.

ROMANIA

SERBIA

YUGO.

BULGARIA

Black Sea

GEORGIA

ANTARCTICA

SPAIN

ANDORRA

ITALY

MACEDONIA

ARMENIA

H

PORTUGAL

ALBANIA

Aegean Sea

TURKEY

AZERBAIJAN

Mediterranean Sea

GREECE

CYPRUS SYRIA

LEBANON

degrees of latitude in the Northern and Southern hemispheres?

55

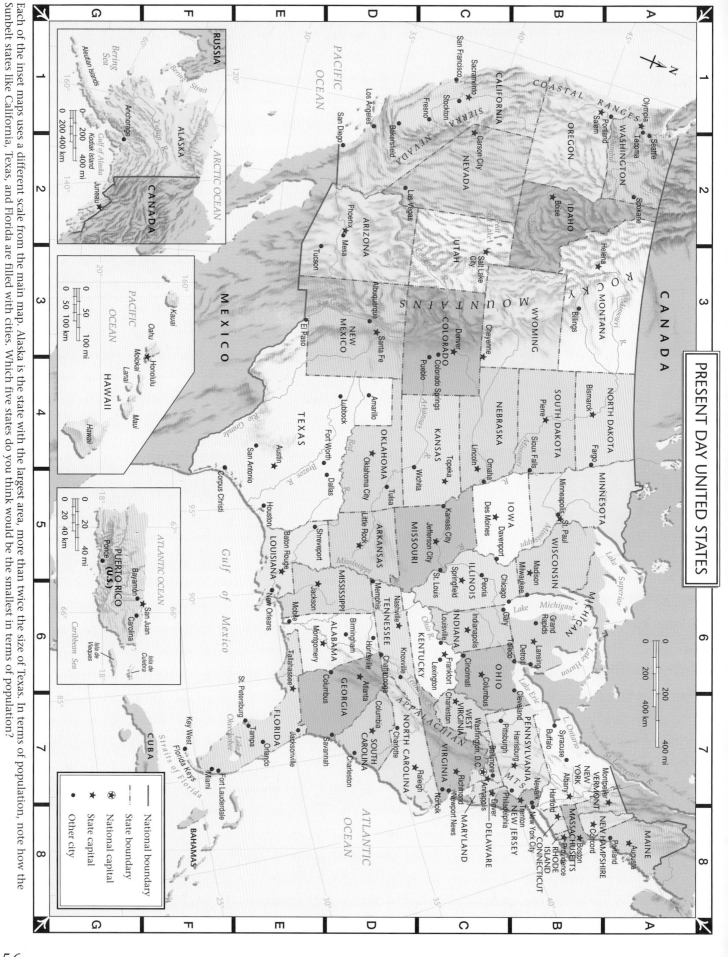

PRESENT DAY UNITED STATES

Each of the inset maps uses a different scale from the main map. Alaska is the state with the largest area, more than twice the size of Texas. In terms of population, note how the Sunbelt states like California, Texas, and Florida are filled with cities. Which five states do you think would be the smallest in terms of population?

Legend:
— National boundary
--- State boundary
⊛ National capital
★ State capital
• Other city

Latin America is composed of the continent of South America, the huge isthmus of Central America which connects North and South America, and the islands of the Caribbean Sea. Which is the largest nation in Latin America, both in terms of area and population? What language is spoken there?

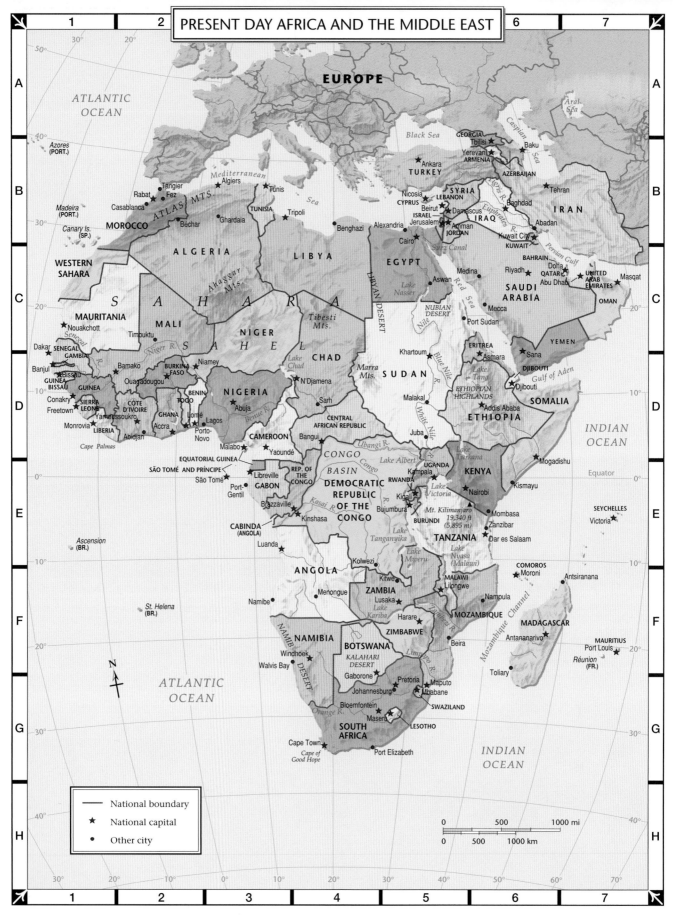

Locate the Sahara, the desert that extends across the northern part of the continent. The region north of the Sahara is often considered part of the Arab World, closely associated with the Middle East. To the South is Sub-Saharan Africa. Which river connects the two regions?

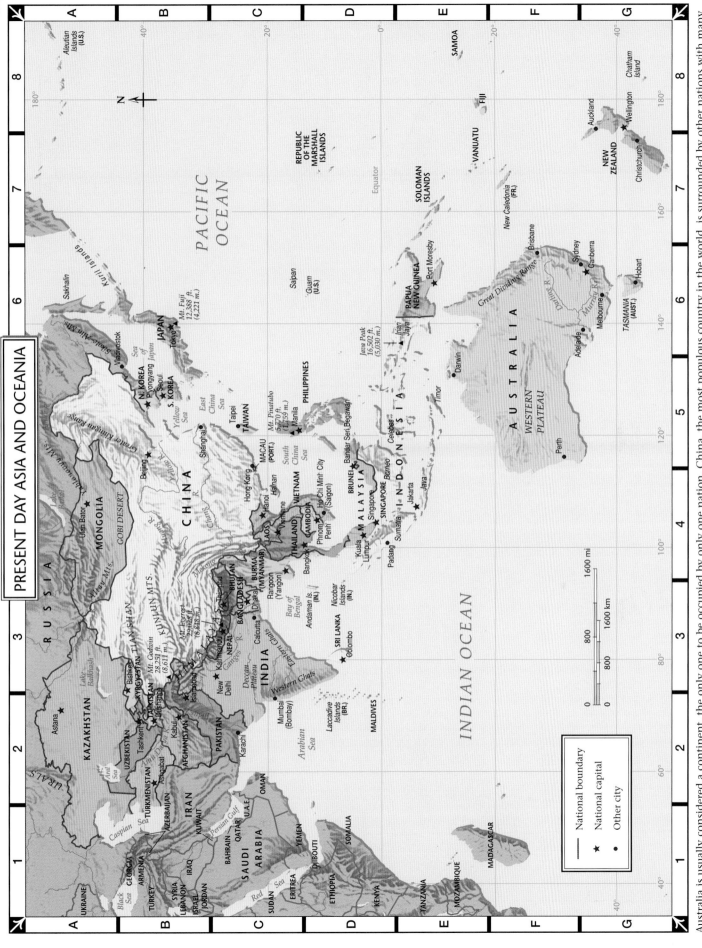

PRESENT DAY ASIA AND OCEANIA

Australia is usually considered a continent, the only one to be occupied by only one nation. China, the most populous country in the world, is surrounded by other nations with many people: India, Indonesia, Japan, Pakistan and Bangladesh. Which nations in Asia and Oceania have capital cites south of the equator?

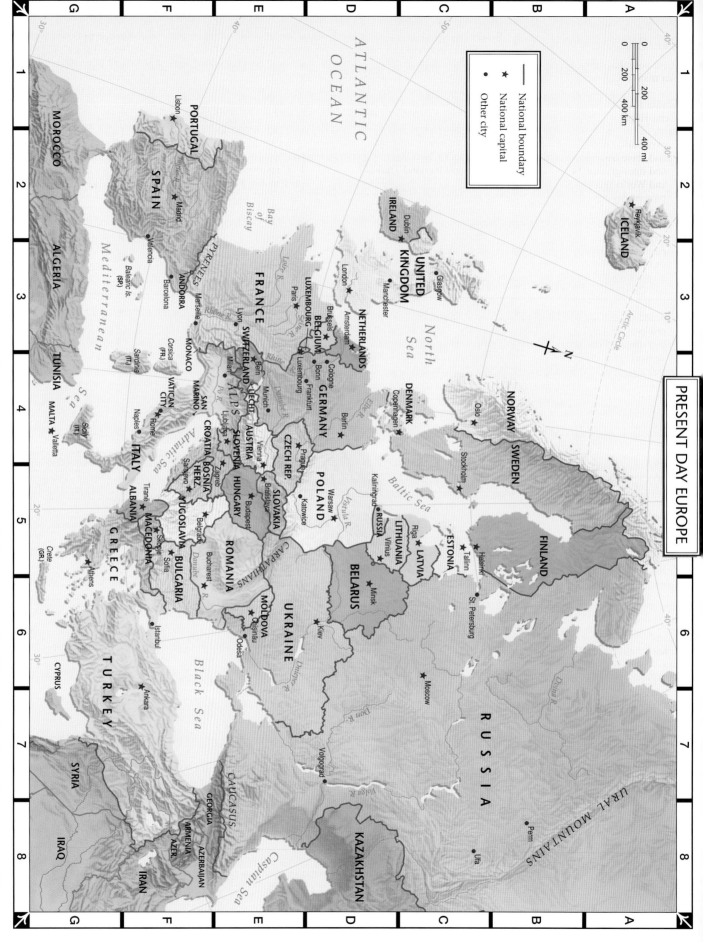

PRESENT DAY EUROPE

It is difficult to say where Europe begins and where Asia ends. Russia, definitely a European nation, extends all the way across Asia. The peninsula called Asia Minor is occupied by Turkey, which is included here as a European nation. What factors might be considered in suggesting an eastern boundary for Europe?

National boundary
★ National capital
• Other city

ATLANTIC
OCEAN

Arctic Circle

ICELAND
★ Reykjavik

NORWAY
★ Oslo

SWEDEN
★ Stockholm

FINLAND
Helsinki ★

North
Sea

Baltic Sea

St. Petersburg •

ESTONIA
Tallinn ★

LATVIA
Riga ★

LITHUANIA
Vilnius ★

Kaliningrad
(RUSSIA) ★

Moscow ★

RUSSIA

Perm •

Ufa •

URAL MOUNTAINS

UNITED
KINGDOM
IRELAND
Dublin ★
• Glasgow
London ★
Manchester •

NETHERLANDS
Amsterdam ★
Brussels ★
BELGIUM
LUXEMBOURG
Luxembourg ★

DENMARK
Copenhagen ★

GERMANY
Bonn ★
Cologne •
Frankfurt •
Berlin ★

POLAND
Warsaw ★
• Katowice

BELARUS
Minsk ★

UKRAINE
Kiev ★

Volgograd •

KAZAKHSTAN

Bay
of
Biscay

FRANCE
Paris ★
Lyon •

PORTUGAL
Lisbon ★

SPAIN
Madrid ★
Valencia •
Barcelona •

Balearic Is.
(SP.)

ANDORRA
Marseille •
MONACO

PYRENEES

Corsica
(FR.)

Sardinia
(IT.)

SWITZERLAND
Bern ★
LIECHT.
Milan •
ALPS
Po R.
ITALY
SAN
MARINO
VATICAN
CITY
Naples •
Rome ★

Sicily
(IT.)

MALTA ★
Valletta

Mediterranean
Sea

MOROCCO

ALGERIA

TUNISIA

Munich •
AUSTRIA
Vienna ★
CZECH REP.
Prague ★
SLOVAKIA
Bratislava ★
HUNGARY
Budapest ★
SLOVENIA
Ljubljana ★
CROATIA
Zagreb ★
BOSNIA
HERZ.
Sarajevo ★
YUGOSLAVIA
Belgrade ★
ROMANIA
Bucharest ★
MOLDOVA
Chişinău ★
Odesa •

Adriatic Sea

ALBANIA
Tiranë ★
MACEDONIA
Skopje ★
BULGARIA
Sofia ★

GREECE

Crete
(GR.)
Athens ★

Black Sea

Istanbul •

CYPRUS

TURKEY
Ankara ★

SYRIA

IRAQ

IRAN

GEORGIA
ARMENIA
AZERBAIJAN
AZER.

CAUCASUS

Caspian Sea

CARPATHIANS

Danube R.

Dnieper R.

Dniester R.

Don R.

Volga R.

Dvina R.

Vistula R.

Elbe R.

Rhine R.

Rhône R.

Loire R.

Seine R.

Douro R.

N

0   200   400 km
0   200   400 mi

INDEX

Please note that references to inset maps are in **bold**.